jQuery Reference Guide

A Comprehensive Exploration of the Popular
JavaScript Library

Jonathan Chaffer

Karl Swedberg

[PACKT] PUBLISHING

BIRMINGHAM - MUMBAI

jQuery Reference Guide

First published: August 2007

Production Reference: 1240707

Published by Packt Publishing Ltd.
32 Lincoln Road
Olton
Birmingham, B27 6PA, UK.

ISBN 978-1-847193-81-0

www.packtpub.com

Cover Image by Karl Swedberg (karl@learningjquery.com)

Credits

Authors

Jonathan Chaffer

Karl Swedberg

Reviewers

Jörn Zaefferer

Dave Methvin

Mike Alsup

Paul Bakaus

Dan Bravender

Senior Acquisition Editor

Douglas Paterson

Development Editor

Nikhil Bangera

Technical Editor

Bansari Barot

Editorial Manager

Dipali Chittar

Project Manager

Patricia Weir

Project Coordinator

Abhijeet Deobhakta

Indexer

Bhushan Pangaonkar

Proofreader

Chris Smith

Production Coordinator

Shantanu Zagade

Cover Designer

Shantanu Zagade

About the Authors

Jonathan Chaffer is the Chief Technology Officer of Structure Interactive, an interactive agency located in Grand Rapids, Michigan. There he oversees web development projects using a wide range of technologies, and continues to collaborate on day-to-day programming tasks as well.

In the open-source community, Jonathan has been very active in the Drupal CMS project, which has adopted jQuery as its JavaScript framework of choice. He is the creator of the Content Construction Kit, a popular module for managing structured content on Drupal sites. He is responsible for major overhauls of Drupal's menu system and developer API reference.

Jonathan lives in Grand Rapids with his wife, Jennifer.

I would like to thank Jenny, who thinks this is wonderful even if it bores her to tears. I'd also like to thank Karl for sharing my love for linguistics, producing a book that hopefully is grammatically immaculate enough to cover up any technical sins.

Karl Swedberg is a web developer at Structure Interactive in Grand Rapids, Michigan, where he spends much of his time implementing design with a focus on web standards—semantic HTML, well-mannered CSS, and unobtrusive JavaScript.

Before his current love affair with web development, Karl worked as a copy editor, a high-school English teacher, and a coffee house owner. His fascination with technology began in the early 1990s when he worked at Microsoft in Redmond, Washington, and it has continued unabated ever since.

Karl's other obsessions include photography, karate, English grammar, and fatherhood. He lives in Grand Rapids with his wife, Sara, and his two children, Benjamin and Lucia.

I wish to thank my wife, Sara, for her steadfast love and support during my far-flung adventures into esoteric nonsense. Thanks also to my two delightful children, Benjamin and Lucia. Jonathan Chaffer has my deepest respect and gratitude for his willingness to write this book with me and to explain the really difficult aspects of programming in a gentle manner when I just don't get it. Finally, I wish to thank John Resig for his brilliant JavaScript library and his ongoing encouragement for the book, as well as Rey Bango, Brandon Aaron, Klaus Hartl, Jörn Zaefferer, Dave Methvin, Mike Alsup, Yehuda Katz, Stefan Petre, Paul Bakaus, Michael Geary, Glen Lipka, and the many others who have provided help and inspiration along the way.

About the Reviewers

Jörn Zaefferer is a software developer and a consultant from Köln, Germany. He is currently working at Maxence Integration Technologies GmbH. His work is centered on developing web-based applications as JSR-168 portlets in JEE environments, mostly Websphere Portal 5.1 based. He is currently working on a project based on JSF and Spring.

Dave Methvin has more than 25 years of software development experience in both the Windows and UNIX environments. His early career focused on embedded software in the fields of robotics, telecommunications, and medicine. Later, he moved to PC-based software projects using C/C++ and web technologies.

Dave also has more than 20 years of experience in computer journalism. He was Executive Editor at *PC Tech Journal* and *Windows Magazine*, covering PC and Internet issues; his how-to columns on JavaScript offered some of the first cut-and-paste solutions to common web page problems. He was also a co-author of the book *Networking Windows NT* (John Wiley & Sons, 1997).

Currently, Dave is Chief Technology Officer at PC Pitstop, a website that helps users fix and optimize the performance of their computers. He is also active in the jQuery community.

Mike Alsup is a Senior Software Developer at ePlus where he works on J2EE and web development projects. He is a graduate from Potsdam College and has been serving the software industry since 1989. Mike lives in Palmyra, NY with his wife, Diane, and their three sons.

His jQuery plug-ins can be found at `http://malsup.com/jquery/`.

Paul Bakaus is a programmer and core developer living in Germany. His work with jQuery has been focused on transforming jQuery into a high-speed library capable of handling difficult large-scale rich interface operations. He was largely responsible for creating the jQuery Dimensions plug-in and he now works together with Stefan Petre on the rich effects and components library Interface. Paul is currently involved in creating a JavaScript multiplayer game featuring jQuery.

Dan Bravender has been working with open-source software for over 10 years. His fondest memories are of staying up all night to install and compile Linux in college with his roommate. He has collected a massive collection of German board games. When not playing board games, he enjoys playing soccer and hockey and studying Korean and Chinese etymology. He misses working with Karl and Jon and is very proud of all the hard work that they put into this book.

Table of Contents

Preface

jQuery is a powerful, yet easy-to-use JavaScript library that helps web developers and designers add dynamic, interactive elements to their sites, smoothing out browser inconsistencies and greatly reducing development time. In *jQuery Reference Guide*, you can investigate this library's features in a thorough, accessible format.

This book offers an organized menu of every jQuery method, function, and selector. Entries are accompanied by detailed descriptions and helpful recipes that will assist you in getting the most out of jQuery and avoiding the pitfalls commonly associated with JavaScript and other client-side languages. If you're still hungry for more, the book shows you how to cook up your own extensions with jQuery's elegant plug-in architecture.

You'll discover the untapped possibilities that jQuery makes available and hone your skills as you return to this guide time and again.

Demos of examples in this book are available at:
`http:\\book.learningjquery.com`.

What This Book Covers

In *Chapter 1* we'll begin by dissecting a working jQuery example. This script will serve as a roadmap for this book, directing you to the chapters containing more information on particular jQuery capabilities.

The heart of the book is a set of reference chapters that allow you to quickly look up the details of any jQuery method. *Chapter 2* lists every available selector for finding page elements.

Chapter 3 builds on the previous chapter with a catalog of jQuery methods for finding page elements.

Chapter 4 describes every opportunity for inspecting and modifying the HTML structure of a page.

Chapter 5 details each event that can be triggered and reacted to by jQuery.

Chapter 6 defines the range of animations built into jQuery, as well as the toolkit available for building your own.

Chapter 7 lists the ways in which jQuery can initiate and respond to server communication without refreshing the page.

Chapter 8 covers the remaining capabilities of the jQuery library that don't neatly fit into the other categories.

In the final three chapters, you'll dive into the extension mechanisms jQuery makes available. *Chapter 9* reveals four major ways to enhance jQuery's already robust capabilities using a plug-in.

Chapter 10 walks you through the advanced measurement tools available in the popular Dimensions plug-in.

Chapter 11 empowers you to bring AJAX technology and HTML forms together, a process which is made easy by the Form plug-in.

Appendix A provides a handful of informative websites on a wide range of topics related to jQuery, JavaScript, and web development in general.

Appendix B recommends a number of useful third-party programs and utilities for editing and debugging jQuery code within your personal development environment.

Who is This Book For?

This book is for web designers who want to create interactive elements for their designs, and for developers who want to create the best user interface for their web applications.

The reader will need the basics of HTML and CSS, and should be comfortable with the syntax of JavaScript. No knowledge of jQuery is assumed, nor is experience with any other JavaScript libraries required.

Conventions

In this book, you will find a number of styles of text that distinguish between different kinds of information. Here are some examples of these styles, and an explanation of their meaning.

There are three styles for code. Code words in text are shown as follows: "Taken together, `$()` and `.addClass()` are enough for us to accomplish our goal of changing the appearance of the poem text."

A block of code will be set as follows:

```
$(document).ready(function() {
  $('span:contains(language)').addClass('emphasized');
});
```

When we wish to draw your attention to a particular part of a code block, the relevant lines or items will be made bold:

```
$(document).ready(function() {
  $('a[@href$=".pdf"]').addClass('pdflink');
});
```

New terms and **important words** are introduced in a bold-type font. Words that you see on the screen, in menus or dialog boxes for example, appear in our text like this: "The next step is to run those tests by clicking the **All** button".

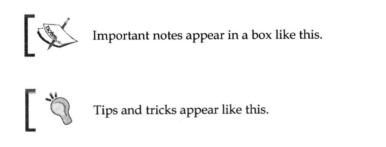

Important notes appear in a box like this.

Tips and tricks appear like this.

Reader Feedback

Feedback from our readers is always welcome. Let us know what you think about this book, what you liked or may have disliked. Reader feedback is important for us to develop titles that you really get the most out of.

To send us general feedback, simply drop an email to `feedback@packtpub.com`, making sure to mention the book title in the subject of your message.

If there is a book that you need and would like to see us publish, please send us a note in the **SUGGEST A TITLE** form on www.packtpub.com or email suggest@packtpub.com.

If there is a topic that you have expertise in and you are interested in either writing or contributing to a book, see our author guide on www.packtpub.com/authors.

Customer Support

Now that you are the proud owner of a Packt book, we have a number of things to help you to get the most from your purchase.

Downloading the Example Code for the Book

Visit http://www.packtpub.com/support, and select this book from the list of titles to download any example code or extra resources for this book. The files available for download will then be displayed.

The downloadable files contain instructions on how to use them.

Errata

Although we have taken every care to ensure the accuracy of our contents, mistakes do happen. If you find a mistake in one of our books—maybe a mistake in text or code—we would be grateful if you would report this to us. By doing this you can save other readers from frustration, and help to improve subsequent versions of this book. If you find any errata, report them by visiting http://www.packtpub.com/support, selecting your book, clicking on the **Submit Errata** link, and entering the details of your errata. Once your errata are verified, your submission will be accepted and the errata added to the list of existing errata. The existing errata can be viewed by selecting your title from http://www.packtpub.com/support.

Questions

You can contact us at questions@packtpub.com if you are having a problem with some aspect of the book, and we will do our best to address it.

Anatomy of a jQuery Script

He's got a brand new start
Now he's a happy guy
                              — Devo,
        "Happy Guy"

A typical jQuery script uses a wide assortment of the methods that the library offers. Selectors, DOM manipulation, event handling, and so forth come into play as required by the task at hand. In order to make the best use of jQuery, we need to keep in mind the wide range of capabilities it provides.

This book will itemize every method and function found in the jQuery library. Since there are many methods and functions to sort through, it will be useful to know what the basic categories of methods are, and how they come into play within a jQuery script. Here we will see a fully functioning script, and examine how the different aspects of jQuery are utilized in each part of the script.

A Dynamic Table of Contents

As an example of jQuery in action, we'll build a small script that will dynamically extract the headings from an HTML document and assemble them into a table of contents for that page.

Our table of contents will be nestled on the top right corner of the page:

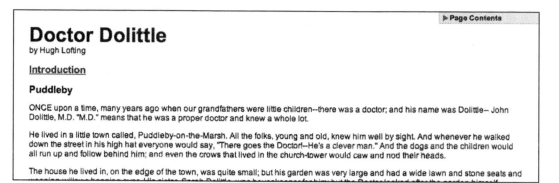

We'll have it collapsed initially as shown above, but a click will expand it to full height:

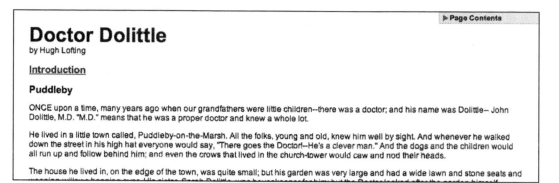

At the same time, we'll add a feature to the main body text. The introduction of the text on the page will not be initially loaded, but when the user clicks on the word **Introduction**, the introductory text will be inserted in place from another file:

> ▶ Page Contents
>
> # Doctor Dolittle
> by Hugh Lofting
>
> TO ALL CHILDREN
> CHILDREN IN YEARS AND CHILDREN IN HEART
> I DEDICATE THIS STORY
>
> There are some of us now reaching middle age who discover themselves to be lamenting the past in one respect if in none other, that there are no books written now for children comparable with those of thirty years ago. I say written FOR children because the new psychological business of writing ABOUT them as though they were small pills or hatched in some especially scientific method is extremely popular today. Writing for children rather than about them is very difficult as everybody who has tried it knows. It can only be done, I am convinced, by somebody having a great deal of the child in his own outlook and sensibilities. Such was the author of "The Little Duke" and "The Dove in the Eagle's Nest," such the author of "A Flatiron for a Farthing," and "The Story of a Short Life." Such, above all, the author of "Alice in Wonderland." Grownups imagine that they can do the trick by adopting baby language and talking down to

Before we reveal the script that performs these tasks, we should walk through the environment in which the script resides.

Obtaining jQuery

The official jQuery website (http://jquery.com/) is always the most up-to-date resource for code and news related to the library. To get started, we need a copy of jQuery, which can be downloaded right from the home page of the site. Several versions of jQuery may be available at any given moment; the latest uncompressed version will be most appropriate for us.

No installation is required for jQuery. To use jQuery, we just need to place it on our site in a public location. Since JavaScript is an interpreted language, there is no compilation or build phase to worry about. Whenever we need a page to have jQuery available, we will simply refer to the file's location from the HTML document.

Setting Up the HTML Document

There are three sections to most examples of jQuery usage— the HTML document itself, CSS files to style it, and JavaScript files to act on it. For this example, we'll use a page containing the text of a book:

```
<?xml version="1.0" encoding="UTF-8" ?>
<!DOCTYPE html PUBLIC "-//W3C//DTD XHTML 1.0 Transitional//EN"
    "http://www.w3.org/TR/xhtml1/DTD/xhtml1-transitional.dtd">

<html xmlns="http://www.w3.org/1999/xhtml" xml:lang="en" lang="en">
  <head>
```

```
    <meta http-equiv="Content-Type" content="text/html;
                                            charset=utf-8"/>
    <title>Doctor Dolittle</title>
     <link rel="stylesheet" href="dolittle.css" type="text/css" />
    <script src="jquery.js" type="text/javascript"></script>
    <script src="dolittle.js" type="text/javascript"></script>
  </head>
  <body>
    <div id="container">
      <h1>Doctor Dolittle</h1>
      <div class="author">by Hugh Lofting</div>
      <div id="introduction">
        <h2><a href="introduction.html">Introduction</a></h2>
      </div>
      <div id="content">
        <h2>Puddleby</h2>
        <p>ONCE upon a time, many years ago when our grandfathers
           were little children--there was a doctor; and his name was
           Dolittle-- John Dolittle, M.D.  &quot;M.D.&quot; means
           that he was a proper doctor and knew a whole lot.
        </p>

        <!-- More text follows... -->

      </div>
    </div>
  </body>
</html>
```

The actual layout of files on the server does not matter. References from one file to another just need to be adjusted to match the organization we choose. In most examples in this book, we will use relative paths to reference files (`../images/foo.png`) rather than absolute paths (`/images/foo.png`). This will allow the code to run locally without the need for a web server.

The stylesheet is loaded immediately after the standard `<head>` elements. Here are the portions of the stylesheet that affect our dynamic elements:

```
/* ----------------------------------
   Page Table of Contents
---------------------------------- */
#page-contents {
  position: absolute;
  text-align: left;
```

```
    top: 0;
    right: 0;
    width: 15em;
    border: 1px solid #ccc;
    border-top-width: 0;
    border-right-width: 0;
    background-color: #e3e3e3;
}
#page-contents h3 {
    margin: 0;
    padding: .25em .5em .25em 15px;
    background: url(arrow-right.gif) no-repeat 0 2px;
    font-size: 1.1em;
    cursor: pointer;
}
#page-contents h3.arrow-down {
    background-image: url(arrow-down.gif);
}
#page-contents a {
    display: block;
    font-size: 1em;
    margin: .4em 0;
    font-weight: normal;
}
#page-contents div {
    padding: .25em .5em .5em;
    display: none;
    background-color: #efefef;
}

/* --------------------
    Introduction
------------------------------------ */
.dedication {
    margin: 1em;
    text-align: center;
    border: 1px solid #555;
    padding: .5em;
}
```

After the stylesheet is referenced, the JavaScript files are included. It is important that the script tag for the jQuery library be placed *before* the tag for our custom scripts; otherwise, the jQuery framework will not be available when our code attempts to reference it.

Writing the jQuery Code

Our custom code will go in the second, currently empty, JavaScript file which we included from the HTML using `<script src="dolittle.js" type="text/javascript"></script>`. Despite how much it accomplishes, the script is fairly short:

```
jQuery.fn.toggleNext = function() {
  this.toggleClass('arrow-down')
    .next().slideToggle('fast');
};


$(document).ready(function() {
  $('<div id="page-contents"></div>')
    .prepend('<h3>Page Contents</h3>')
    .append('<div></div>')
    .prependTo('body');

  $('#content h2').each(function(index) {
    var $chapterTitle = $(this);
    var chapterId = 'chapter-' + (index + 1);
    $chapterTitle.attr('id', chapterId);
    $('<a></a>').text($chapterTitle.text())
      .attr({
        'title': 'Jump to ' + $chapterTitle.text(),
        'href': '#' + chapterId
      })
      .appendTo('#page-contents div');
  });

  $('#page-contents h3').click(function() {
    $(this).toggleNext();
  });

  $('#introduction > h2 a').click(function() {
    $('#introduction').load(this.href);
    return false;
  });
});
```

We now have a dynamic table of contents that brings users to the relevant portion of the text, and an introduction that is loaded on demand.

Script Dissection

This script has been chosen specifically because it illustrates the widespread capabilities of the jQuery library. Now that we've seen the code as a whole, we can identify the categories of methods used therein.

 We will not discuss the operation of this script in much detail here, but a similar script is presented as a tutorial on the Learning jQuery web log: `http://www.learningjquery.com/2007/06/automatic-page-contents`.

Selector Expressions

Before we can act on an HTML document, we need to locate the relevant portions. In our script, we sometimes use a simple approach to finding an element:

```
$('#introduction')
```

This expression creates a new jQuery object that references the element with the ID introduction. On the other hand, sometimes we require a more intricate selector:

```
$('#introduction > h2 a')
```

Here we produce a jQuery object potentially referring to many elements. Elements are included if they are anchor tags, but only if they are descendants of `<h2>` elements that are themselves children of an element with the ID introduction.

These **selector expressions** can be as simple or complex as we need. Chapter 2 will enumerate all of the selectors available to us and how they can be combined.

DOM Traversal Methods

Sometimes we have a jQuery object that already references a set of DOM elements, but we need to perform an action on a different, related set of elements. In these cases, **DOM traversal** methods are useful. We can see this in part of our script:

```
this.toggleClass('arrow-down')
  .next()
  .slideToggle('fast');
```

Because of the context of this piece of code, the keyword `this` refers to a jQuery object (it often refers instead to a DOM element). In our case, this jQuery object is in turn pointing to the `<h3>` heading of the table of contents. The `.toggleClass` method call manipulates this heading element. The subsequent `.next()` operation changes the element we are working with, though, so that the following `.slideToggle` method call acts on the `<div>` containing the table of contents rather than its header. The methods that allow us to freely move about the DOM tree like this are listed in Chapter 3.

DOM Manipulation Methods

Finding elements is not enough; we want to be able to change them as well. Such changes can be as straightforward as changing a single attribute:

```
$chapterTitle.attr('id', chapterId);
```

Here we modify the ID of the matched element on the fly.

Sometimes the changes are further-reaching, on the other hand:

```
$('<div id="page-contents"></div>')
  .prepend('<h3>Page Contents</h3>')
  .append('<div></div>')
  .prependTo('body');
```

This part of the script illustrates that the **DOM manipulation** methods can not only alter elements in place, but also remove, shuffle, and insert them. These lines add a new heading at the beginning of `<div id="page-contents">`, insert another `<div>` container at the end of it, and place the whole thing at the beginning of the document body. Chapter 4 will detail these and many more ways to modify the DOM tree.

Event Methods

Even when we can modify the page at will, our pages will sit in place, unresponsive. We need **event methods** to react to user input, making our changes at the appropriate time:

```
$('#introduction > h2 a').click(function() {
  $('#introduction').load(this.href);
  return false;
});
```

In this snippet we register a handler that will execute each time the selected anchor tag is clicked. The click event is one of the most common ones observed, but there are many others; the jQuery methods that interact with them are discussed in Chapter 5.

Chapter 5 also discusses a very special event method, `.ready`:

```
$(document).ready(function() {
  // ...
});
```

This method allows us to register behavior that will occur immediately when the structure of the DOM is available to our code—even before the images have loaded.

Effect Methods

The event methods allow us to react to user input; the **effect methods** let us do this with style. Instead of immediately hiding and showing elements, we can do so with an animation:

```
this.toggleClass('arrow-down')
  .next()
  .slideToggle('fast');
```

This method performs a fast sliding transition on the element, alternately hiding and showing it with each invocation. The built-in effect methods are listed in Chapter 6, as is the way to create new ones.

AJAX Methods

Many modern websites employ techniques to load content when requested without a page refresh; jQuery allows us to accomplish this with ease. The **AJAX Methods** initiate these content requests and allow us to monitor their progress:

```
$('#introduction > h2 a').click(function() {
  $('#introduction').load(this.href);
  return false,
});
```

Here the `.load` method allows us to get another HTML document from the server and insert it in the current document, all with one line of code. This and more sophisticated mechanisms of retrieving information from the server are listed in Chapter 7.

Miscellaneous Methods

Some methods are harder to classify than others. The jQuery library incorporates several **miscellaneous methods** that serve as shorthand for common JavaScript idioms.

Even basic tasks like iteration are simplified by jQuery:

```
$('#content h2').each(function(index) {
  // ...
});
```

The `.each` method seen here steps through the matched elements in turn, performing the enclosed code on all of matched elements. In this case, the method helps us to collect all of the headings on the page so that we can assemble a complete table of contents. More helper functions such as this can be found in Chapter 8.

Plug-In API

We need not confine ourselves to built-in functionality either. The **plug-in API** that is part of jQuery allows us to augment the capabilities already present with new ones that suit our needs. Even in the small script we've written here, we've found the use for a plug-in:

```
jQuery.fn.toggleNext = function() {
  this.toggleClass('arrow-down')
    .next().slideToggle('fast');
};
```

This code defines a new `.toggleNext` jQuery method that slides the following element open and shut. We can now call our new method later when needed:

```
$('#page-contents h3').click(function() {
  $(this).toggleNext();
});
```

Whenever code could be reused outside the current script, it might do well as a plug-in. Chapter 9 will cover the plug-in API used to build these extensions.

Summary

We've now seen a complete, functional jQuery-powered script. This example, though small, brings a significant amount of interactivity and usability to the page. The script has illustrated the major types of tools offered by jQuery, as well. We've observed how the script finds items in the DOM and changes them as necessary. We've witnessed response to user action, and animation to give feedback to the user after the action. We've even seen how to pull information from the server without a page refresh, and how to teach jQuery brand new tricks in the form of plug-ins.

We'll be stepping through each function, method, and selector expression in the jQuery library now, chapter by chapter. In illustrating many of them, a customized logging function will aid our examples. This `.log` method prints text to the screen in a useful context; we'll dissect it as an example of a plug-in at the end of Chapter 9.

Each method will be introduced with a summary of its syntax and a list of its parameters and return value. Then we will offer a discussion, which will provide examples where applicable. For further reading about any method, consult the online resources listed in Appendix A.

2

Selector Expressions

You got me lookin' up high
You got me searchin' down low
                    — Devo,
        "Jerkin' Back 'n' Forth"

Borrowing from CSS 1–3 and basic XPath, and then adding its own, jQuery offers a powerful set of selector expressions for matching a set of elements in a document. In this chapter, we'll examine every selector expression that jQuery makes available in turn.

CSS Selectors

The following selectors are based on the CSS 1–3, as outlined by the W3C. For more information about the specifications, visit `http://www.w3.org/Style/CSS/#specs`.

Element: T

All elements that have a tag name of T.

Example

1. `$('div')`: selects all elements with a tag name of div in the document
2. `$('em')`: selects all elements with a tag name of em in the document

Description

jQuery uses JavaScript's `getElementsByTagName()` function for tag-name selectors.

ID: #myid

The unique element with an ID equal to myid.

Examples

1. `$('#myid')`: selects the unique element with `id='myid'`, regardless of its tag name

2. `$('p#myid')`: selects a single paragraph with an `id` of `'myid'`; in other words, the unique element `<p id='myid'>`

Description

Each `id` value must be used only once within a document. If more than one element has been assigned the same `id`, queries that use that `id` will only select the first matched element in the DOM.

It might not be immediately clear why someone might want to specify a tag name associated with a particular `id`, since that `id` needs to be unique anyway. However, some situations in which parts of the DOM are user-generated may require a more specific expression to avoid false positives. Furthermore, when the same script is run on more than one page, it might be necessary to identify the `id`'s element, since the pages could be associating the same `id` with different elements. For example, Page A might have `<h1 id='title'>` while Page B has `<h2 id='title'>`.

For a plain `id` selector such as example 2 above, jQuery uses the JavaScript function `getElementById()`. If the script's execution speed is paramount, the plain `id` selector should be used.

Class: .myclass

All elements that have a class of `myclass`.

Examples

1. `$('.myclass')`: selects all elements that have a class of `myclass`

2. `$('p.myclass')`: selects all paragraphs that have a class of `myclass`

3. `$('.myclass.otherclass')`: selects all elements that have a class of `myclass` and `otherclass`

Description

In terms of speed, example 2 is generally preferable to example 1 (if we can limit the query to a given tag name) because it first uses the native JavaScript function `getElementsByTagName()` to filter its search, and then looks for the class within the matched subset of DOM elements. Conversely, there is currently no native `getElementsByClassName()` for jQuery to use, so using a bare class name forces jQuery to match it against every element in the DOM. The difference in speed varies, however, with the complexity of the page and the number of DOM elements.

As always, remember that development time is typically the most valuable resource. Do not focus on optimization of selector speed unless it is clear that performance needs to be improved.

As a CSS selector, the multiple-class syntax of example 3 is supported by all modern web browsers, but *not* by Internet Explorer versions 6 and below, which makes the syntax especially handy for applying styles cross-browser through jQuery.

Descendant: E F

All elements matched by F that are descendants of an element matched by E.

Examples

1. `$('#container p')`: selects all elements matched by `<p>` that are descendants of an element that has an id of `container`

2. `$('a img')`: selects all elements matched by `<img>` that are descendants of an element matched by `<a>`

Description

A descendant of an element could be a child, grandchild, great-grandchild, and so on, of that element. For example, in the following HTML, the `<img>` element is a descendant of the `<span>`, `<p>`, `<div id="inner">`, and `<div id="container">` elements:

```
<div id="container">
  <div id="inner">
    <p>
      <span><img src="example.jpg" alt="" /></span>
    </p>
  </div>
</div>
```

Child: E > F

All elements matched by F that are children of an element matched by E.

Examples

1. `$('li > ul')`: selects all elements matched by `<ul>` that are children of an element matched by `<li>`

2. `$('p > code')`: selects all elements matched by `<code>` that are children of an element matched by `<p>`

Description

As a CSS selector, the child combinator is supported by all modern web browsers including Safari, Mozilla/Firefox, and Internet Explorer 7, but notably *not* by Internet Explorer versions 6 and below. Example 1 is a handy way to select all nested unordered lists (i.e. excepting the top level).

The child combinator can be thought of as a more specific form of the (single-space) descendant combinator in that it selects only first-level descendants. Therefore, in the following HTML, the `<img>` element is a child only of the `<span>` element.

```
<div id="container">
  <div id="inner">
    <p>
      <span><img src="example.jpg" alt="" /></span>
    </p>
  </div>
</div>
```

Adjacent Sibling: E + F

All elements matched by F that *immediately* follow, and have the same parent as, an element matched by E.

Examples

1. `$('ul + p')`: selects all elements by `<p>` (paragraph) that immediately follow a sibling element matched by `<ul>` (unordered list)

2. `$('strong + em')`: selects all elements matched by `<em>` that immediately follow a sibling element matched by `<strong>`

Description

One important point to consider with both the + combinator and the ~ combinator (covered next) is that they only select siblings. Consider the following HTML:

```
<div id="container">
  <ul>
    <li></li>
    <li></li>
  </ul>
  <p>
    <img/>
  </p>
</div>
```

`$('ul + p')` selects `<p>` because it immediately follows `<ul>` and the two elements share the same parent, `<div id="container">`.

`$('ul + img')` selects nothing because (among other reasons) `<ul>` is one level higher in the DOM tree than `<img>`.

`$('li + img')` selects nothing because, even though `<li>` and `<img>` are on the same level in the DOM tree, they do not share the same parent.

General Sibling: E ~ F

All elements matched by F that follow, and have the same parent as, an element matched by E.

Examples

1. `$('p ~ ul')`: selects all elements matched by `<ul>` that follow a sibling element matched by `<p>`
2. `$('code ~ code')`: selects all elements matched by `<code>` that follow a sibling element matched by `<code>`

Description

One important point to consider with both the + combinator and the ~ combinator is that they only select *siblings*. The notable difference between the two is their respective reach. While the + combinator reaches only to the *immediately* following sibling element, the ~ combinator extends that reach to *all* following sibling elements.

Consider the following HTML:

```
<ul>
  <li class="first"></li>
  <li class="second"></li>
  <li class="third></li>
</ul>
<ul>
  <li class="fourth"></li>
  <li class="fifth"></li>
  <li class="sixth"></li>
</ul>
```

`$('li.first ~ li')` selects `<li class="second">` and `<li class="third">`.

`$('li.first + li')` selects `<li class="second">`.

Multiple Elements: E,F,G

Selects all elements matched by selector expressions E, F, or G.

Examples

1. `$('code, em, strong')`: selects all elements matched by `<code>` or `<em>` or `<strong>`

2. `$('p strong, .myclass')`: selects all elements matched by `<strong>` that are descendants of an element matched by `<p>` as well as all elements that have a class of `myclass`

Description

This comma (,) combinator is an efficient way to select disparate elements. An alternative to this combinator is the `.add()` method described in Chapter 3.

Nth Child (:nth-child(n))

All elements that are the nth child of their parent.

Examples

1. `$('li:nth-child(2)')`: selects all elements matched by `<li>` that are the second child of their parent

2. `$('p:nth-child(5)')`: selects all elements matched by `<p>` that are the fifth child of their parent

Description

Because jQuery's implementation of `:nth-child(n)` is strictly derived from the CSS specification, the value of n is *1-based*, meaning that the counting starts at 1. For all other selector expressions, however, jQuery follows JavaScript's "0-based" counting. Therefore, given a single `<ul>` containing two `<li>`s, `$('li:nth-child(1)')` selects the first `<li>` while `$('li:nth(1)')` selects the second.

Because the two look so similar, the `:nth-child(n)` pseudo-class is easily confused with `:nth(n)`, even though, as we have just seen, the two can result in dramatically different matched elements. With `:nth-child(n)`, all children are counted, regardless of what they are, and the specified element is selected only if it matches the selector attached to the pseudo-class. With `:nth(n)` only the selector attached to the pseudo-class is counted, not limited to children of any other element, and the nth one is selected. To demonstrate this distinction, let's examine the results of a few selector expressions given the following HTML:

```
<div>
  <h2></h2>
```

```
    <p></p>
    <h2></h2>
    <p></p>
    <p></p>
</div>
```

`$('p:nth(1)')` selects the second `<p>`, because numbering for `:nth(n)` starts with 0.

`$('p:nth-child(1)')` selects nothing, because there is no `<p>` element that is the first child of its parent.

`$('p:nth(2)')` selects the third `<p>`.

`$('p:nth-child(2)')` selects the first `<p>`, because it is the second child of its parent.

In addition to taking an integer, `:nth-child(n)` can take even or odd. This makes it especially useful for table-row striping solutions when more than one table appears in a document. Again, given the HTML snippet above:

`$('p:nth-child(even)')` selects the first and third `<p>`, because they are children 2 and 4 (both even numbers) of their parent.

First Child (:first-child)

All elements that are the first child of their parent:

Examples

1. `$('li:first-child')`: selects all elements matched by `<li>` that are the first child of their parent

2. `$(strong:first-child')`: selects all elements matched by `<strong>` that are the first child of their parent

Description

The `:first-child` pseudo-class is shorthand for `:nth-child(1)`. For more information on `:X-child` pseudo-classes, see the discussion for `:nth-child(n)`.

Last Child (:last-child)

All elements that are the last child of their parent.

Examples

1. `$('li:last-child')`: selects all elements matched by `<li>` that are the last child of their parent

2. `$('code:last-child')`: selects all elements matched by `<code>` that are the last child of their parent

Description

For more information on `:X-child` pseudo-classes, see the discussion for `:nth-child(n)`.

Only Child :only-child

All elements that are the only child of their parent.

Examples

1. `$(':only-child')`: selects all elements that are the only child of their parent
2. `$('code:only-child')`: selects all elements matched by `<code>` that are the only child of their parent

Not :not(s)

All elements that do not match selector s.

Examples

1. `$('li:not(.myclass)')`: selects all elements matched by `<li>` that do not have `class="myclass"`
2. `$('li:not(:last-child)')`: selects all elements matched by `<li>` that are not the last child of their parent element

Empty :empty

All elements that have no children (including text nodes).

Examples

1. `$(':empty')`: selects all elements that have no children
2. `$('p:empty')`: selects all elements matched by `<p>` that have no children

Description

The W3C recommends that the `<p>` element have at least one child node, even if that child is merely text (see `http://www.w3.org/TR/html401/struct/text.html#edef-P`). Some other elements, on the other hand, are empty (i.e. have no children) by definition: `<input>`, `<img>`, `<br>`, and `<hr>`, for example.

One important thing to note with `:empty` (and `:parent`) is that *child elements include text nodes.*

Universal: *

All elements.

Examples

1. `$('*')`: selects all elements in the document
2. `$('p > *')`: selects all elements that are children of a paragraph element

Description

The * selector is especially useful when combined with other elements to form a more specific selector expression.

XPath Selectors

Modeled after a file system's directory-tree navigation, XPath selector expressions provide an alternative way to access DOM elements. Although XPath was developed as a selector language for XML documents, jQuery makes a basic subset of its selectors available for use in XML and HTML documents alike.

For more information about XPath 1.0, visit the specification at the W3C: `http://www.w3.org/TR/xpath`.

Descendant: E//F

All elements matched by F that are descendants of an element matched by E.

Examples

1. `$('div//code')`: selects all elements matched by `<code>` that are descendants of an element matched by `<div>`
2. `$('//p//a')`: selects all elements matched by `<a>` that are descendants of an element matched by `<p>`

Description

This XPath descendant selector works the same as the corresponding CSS descendant selector (`$('E F')`) except that the XPath version can specify that it is to start at the document root, which could be useful when querying an XML document.

In example 2, the initial `//p` tells jQuery to start at the document root and match all `<p>` elements that are descendants of it. Keep in mind that if this selector expression follows a DOM traversal method such as `.find()`, this syntax will not select anything because the document root cannot be a child of anything else. Since jQuery allows free mixing of CSS and XPath selectors, the initial `//` is redundant and, therefore, can be omitted.

Child: E/F

All elements matched by F that are children of an element matched by E.

Examples

1. `$('div/p')`: selects all elements matched by `<p>` that are children of an element matched by `<div>`

2. `$('p/a')`: selects all elements matched by `<a>` that are children of an element matched by `<p>`

3. `$('/docroot/el')`: selects all elements matched by `<el>` that are children of an element matched by `<docroot>`, as long as `<docroot>` is actually at the document root

Description

The XPath child selector, `$('E/F')`, is an alternative to the CSS child selector, `$('E > F')`. If the selector expression begins with a single slash, as is the case in example 3, the selector immediately following the slash must be at the document root. Beginning with a single slash is not recommended in HTML documents, since it always must be followed with `body` for the expression to match any elements on the page. For XML documents, however, it might be useful to identify a particular element or attribute at the document root.

Parent: E/..

All elements that are parents of an element matched by E.

Examples

1. `$('.myclass/..')`: selects the parent element of all elements that have a class of `myclass`

2. `$('.myclass/../')`: selects all elements that are children of the parent of an element that has a class of `myclass`. In other words, it selects all elements that have a class of `myclass`, along with their sibling elements

3. `$('.myclass/../p')`: selects all elements matched by `<p>` that are children of the element that has a class of `myclass`

Description

Let's look at some sample HTML to help understand this one:

```
<div>
  <p id="firstp"></p>
  <div id="subdiv"></div>
  <p id="secondp">
```

```
        <span class="myclass"></span>
    </p>
</div>
<div>
    <p></p>
</div>
```

`$('span.myclass/..')` selects `<p id="secondp">`, because it is the parent of `<span class="myclass">`.

`$('#firstp/../')` selects `<p id="firstp">`, `<div id="subdiv">`, and `<p id="secondp">`, because the selector (a) starts with `<p id="firstp">`, (b) traverses up one level in the DOM tree (to the first top-level `<div>` element), and (c) selects all children of that `<div>`.

`$('.myclass/../../p')` selects `<p id="firstp">` and `<p id="secondp">`, because the selector (a) starts with `<span class="myclass">`, (b) traverses up two levels in the DOM tree (to the first top-level `<div>` element), and (c) selects all `<p>` elements that are children of that `<div>`.

Contains: [F]

All elements that contain an element matched by F.

Examples

1. `$('div[p]')`: selects all elements matched by `<div>` that contain an element matched by `<p>`
2. `$('p[.myclass]')`: selects all elements matched by `<p>` that contain an element with a class of `myclass`

Description

This selector is like the reverse of the descendant selector (either E//F or E F), in that it selects all elements that have a descendant element matched by F instead of all elements matched by F that are descendants of some other element.

The XPath *contains* selector is not to be confused with the CSS *attribute* selector, which shares this syntax. jQuery uses the XPath-style expression for attribute selectors too, as discussed in the *Attribute Selectors* section below.

Attribute Selectors

Because jQuery supports both CSS and XPath-style expressions and the two conflict in their use of square brackets, jQuery adopts the XPath notation for attribute selectors, beginning them with the @ symbol.

When using any of the following attribute selectors, we should account for attributes that have multiple, space-separated values. Since these selectors see attribute values as a single string, this selector, for example, `$('[a@rel=nofollow]')`, will select `<a rel="nofollow" href="example.html">Some text</a>` but *not* `<a rel="nofollow self" href="example.html">Some text</a>`.

Attribute values in selector expressions can be written as bare words or surrounded by quotation marks. Therefore, the following variations are equally correct:

- bare words: `$('[a@rel=nofollow self]')`
- double quotes inside single quotes: `$('[a@rel="nofollow self"]')`
- single quotes inside double quotes: `$("[a@rel='nofollow self']")`
- escaped single quotes inside single quotes:
  `$('[a@rel=\'nofollow self\']')`
- escaped double quotes inside double quotes:
  `$("[a@rel=\"nofollow self\"]")`

The variation we choose is generally a matter of style or convenience.

Has Attribute: [@foo]

All elements that have the `foo` attribute.

Examples

1. `$('a[@rel]')`: selects all elements matched by `<a>` that have a `rel` attribute
2. `$('p[@class]')`: selects all elements matched by `<p>` that have a `class` attribute

Description

For more information on this attribute selector, see the introduction to *Attribute Selectors* above.

Attribute Value Equals: [@foo=bar]

Elements that have the `foo` attribute with a value exactly equal to `bar`.

Examples

1. `$('a[@rel=nofollow]')`: selects all elements matched by `<a>` that have a `rel` value exactly equal to `nofollow`
2. `$('input[@name=myname]')`: selects all elements matched by `<input>` that have a `name` value exactly equal to `myname`

Description

For more information on this attribute selector, see the introduction to *Attribute Selectors* above.

Attribute Value Does Not Equal: [@foo!=bar]

All elements that do *not* have the `foo` attribute with a value exactly equal to `bar`.

Examples

1. `$('a[@rel!=nofollow]')`: selects all elements matched by `<a>` that do not have a `rel` attribute with a value exactly equal to `nofollow`

2. `$('input[@name!=myname]')`: selects all elements matched by `<input>` that do not have a `name` attribute with a value exactly equal to `myname`

Description

Since these selectors see attribute values as a single string, `$('[a@rel!=nofollow]')` we *will* select `<a rel="nofollow self" href="example.htm">Some text</a>`.

If we need to select only `<a>` elements that do not have `nofollow` anywhere within their `rel` attribute, we can use the following selector expression instead: `$('a:not([@rel*=nofollow])')`.

Attribute Value Begins: [@foo^=bar]

All elements that have the `foo` attribute with a value *beginning* exactly with the string `bar`.

Examples

1. `$('a[@rel^=no]')`: selects all elements matched by `<a>` that have a `rel` attribute value beginning with `no`

2. `$('input[@name^=my]')`: selects all elements matched by `<input>` that have a `name` value beginning with `my`

Description

Since these selectors see attribute values as a single string, `$('[a@rel^=no]')` will select `<a rel="nofollow self" href="example.htm">Some text</a>` but *not* `<a rel="self nofollow" href="example.htm">Some text</a>`.

Attribute Value Ends: [@foo$=bar]

All elements that have the `foo` attribute with a value ending exactly with the string `bar`.

Examples

1. `$('a[@href$=index.htm]')`: selects all elements matched by `<a>` that have an `href` value ending with `index.htm`

2. `$('a[@rel$=self]')`: selects all elements matched by `<p>` that have a `class` value ending with `bar`

Description

Since these selectors see attribute values as a single string, `$('[a@rel$=self]')` will select `<a rel="nofollow self" href="example.htm">Some text</a>` but *not* `<a rel="self nofollow" href="example.htm">Some text</a>`.

Attribute Value Contains: [@foo*=bar]

All elements that have the `foo` attribute with a value *containing* the substring `bar`.

Examples

1. `$('p[@class*=bar]')`: selects all elements matched by `<p>` that have a `class` value containing `bar`

2. `$('a[@href*=example.com]')`: selects all elements matched by `<a>` that have an `href` value containing `example.com`

Description

This is the most generous selector of the jQuery attribute selectors that match against a value. It will select an element if the selector's string appears anywhere within the element's attribute value. Therefore, `$('p[@class*=my]')` will select `<p class="yourclass myclass">Some text</p>`, `<p class="myclass yourclass">Some text</p>`, *and* `<p class="thisismyclass">Some text</p>`.

Form Selectors

The following selectors can be used to access form elements in a variety of states. When using any of the form selectors other than `:input`, providing a tag name as well is recommended (for example, `input:text`, rather than `:text`).

- All form elements (`<input>` (all types), `<select>`, `<textarea>`, `<button>`)
- All text fields (`<input type="text">`)

- All password fields (`<input type="password">`)
- All radio fields (`<input type="radio">`)
- All checkbox fields (`<input type="checkbox">`)
- All submit inputs and button elements (`<input type="submit">`, `<button>`)
- All image inputs (`<input type="image">`)
- All reset buttons (`<input type="reset">`)
- All button elements and input elements with a type of `button` (`<button>`, `<input type="button">`)
- All user interface elements that are enabled
- All user interface elements that are disabled
- All user interface element — checkboxes and radio buttons — that are checked
- All elements, including `<input type="hidden" />`, that are hidden

For more information, see the discussion on `:hidden` in the *Custom Selectors* section below.

Custom Selectors

The following selectors were added to the jQuery library as an attempt to address common DOM traversal needs not met by either CSS or basic XPath.

Even Element (:even) Odd Element (:odd)

All elements with an even index:

    :even

All elements with an odd index:

    :odd

Examples

1. `$('li:even')`: selects all elements matched by `<li>` that have an even index value
2. `$('tr:odd')`: selects all elements matched by `<tr>` that have an odd index value

Description

Because the custom :even and :odd pseudo-classes match elements based on their index, they use JavaScript's native zero-based numbering.

Somewhat counter-intuitively, therefore, :even selects the first, third, fifth (and so on) elements while :odd selects the second, fourth, sixth (and so on) elements.

The one exception to this rule is the :nth-child(n) selector, which is one-based. So, :nth-child(even) selects the second, fourth, sixth (and so on) child element of its parent. Also worth noting is the lack of a colon preceding even or odd when used with :nth-child().

Nth Element (:eq(n), :nth(n))

The element with index value equal to n.

Examples

1. $('li:eq(2)'): selects the third <li> element
2. $('p:nth(1)'): selects the second <p> element

Description

Because the JavaScript index is zero-based, :eq(0) and :nth(0) select the first matched element, :eq(1) and :nth(1) select the second, and so on.

Greater Than :gt(n)

All elements with index greater than N.

Examples

1. $('li:gt(1)'): selects all elements matched by <li> after the second one
2. $('a:gt(2)'): selects all elements matched by <a> after the third one

Description

Because the JavaScript index is zero-based, :gt(1) selects all matched elements beginning with the third one, :gt(2) selects all matched elements beginning with the fourth, and so on. Consider the following HTML:

```
<ul>
  <li id="first">index 0</li>
  <li id="second">index 1</li>
  <li id="third">index 2</li>
  <li id="fourth">index 3</li>
</ul>
```

`$('li:gt(1)')` selects `<li id="third">` and `<li id="fourth">`, because their indexes are greater than 1.

`$(li:gt(2)')` selects `<li id="fourth">`, because its index is greater than 2.

Less Than : lt(n)

All elements with index less than N.

Examples

1. `$('li:lt(2)')`: selects all elements matched by `<li>` element before the third one; in other words, the first two `<li>` elements

2. `$('p:lt(3)')`: selects all elements matched by `<p>` elements before the fourth one; in other words the first three `<p>` elements

Description

Because the JavaScript index is zero-based, `:lt(2)` selects the first two matched elements, or all matched element before the third one; `:lt(3)` selects the first three matched elements, or all matched elements before the fourth; and so on.

First :first

The first instance of an element.

Examples

1. `$('li:first')`: selects the first `<li>` element

2. `$('a:first')`: selects the first `<a>` element

Discussion

The `:first` pseudo-class is shorthand for `:eq(0)`. It could also be written as `:lt(1)`.

Last :last

The last instance of an element.

Examples

1. `$('li:last)`: selects the last `<li>` element

2. `$('#container .myclass:last)`: selects the last element that has a class of `myclass` and is a descendant of the element with an `id` of `container`

Description

While :first has equivalent selectors (nth(0) and eq(0)) the :last pseudo-class is unique in its ability to select only the last element in the set of matched elements.

Parent :parent

All elements that are the parent of another element, including text.

Examples

1. $(':parent'): selects all elements that are the parent of another element, including text
2. $(td:parent'): selects all elements matched by `<td>` that are the parent of another element, including text

Description

The W3C recommends that the `<p>` element have at least one child node, even if that child is merely text (see http://www.w3.org/TR/html401/struct/text.html#edef P). For example, some elements, on the other hand, are empty (i.e. have no children) by definition: `<input>`, `<img>`, `<br>`, and `<hr>`.

One important thing to note with :parent (and :empty) is that child elements include text nodes.

Contains :contains(text)

All elements that contain the specified text.

Examples

1. $('p:contains(nothing special)'): selects all elements matched by `<p>` that contain the text nothing special
2. $('li:contains(second)'): selects all elements matched by `<li>` that contain the text second

Description

The matching text can appear in the selector element or in any of that element's descendants. Therefore, example 1 would still select the following paragraph:

```
<p>This paragraph is <span>nothing <strong>special</strong>
                                               </span></p>
```

As with attribute value selectors, text inside the parentheses of :contains() can be written as bare words or surrounded by quotation marks. Also, the text must have matching case to be selected.

Visible :visible

All elements that are visible.

Examples

1. `$('li:visible')`: selects all elements matched by `<li>` that are visible
2. `$('input:visible')`: selects all elements matched by `<input>` that are visible

Discussion

The :visible selector includes items that have a display of block or inline (or any other value other than none) and a visibility of visible. Form elements that have type="hidden" are excluded.

It's important to note that elements will be selected by the :visible pseudo-class even if their parent (or other ancestor) element has a display of none, as long as they themselves have a display of block or inline (or any other value other than none). Therefore, it's possible for an element to be hidden from view but still be selected by :visible.

Consider the following HTML:

```
<div id="parent" style="display:none">
  <div id="child" style="display:block">
  </div>
</div>
```

Although `<div id="child">` is not visible on the web page because of its parent `<div>`'s display property, it is still selected by `$('div:visible')`.

Hidden :hidden

All elements that are hidden

Examples

1. `$('li:hidden)`: selects all elements matched by `<li>` that are hidden
2. `$('input:hidden)`: selects all elements matched by `<input>` that are hidden

Description

The :hidden selector includes elements that have a CSS declaration of display: none or visibility:hidden, as well as form elements with type="hidden".

If an element is hidden from view only because its parent (or other ancestor) element has a display of none or visibility of hidden, it will not be selected by :hidden when its own display property isn't none and its visibility property isn't hidden.

Consider the following HTML:

```
<div id="parent" style="display:none">
  <div id="child" style="display:block">
  </div>
</div>
```

Although the child <div> is not visible on the web page because of its parent <div>'s display property, $('div:hidden') only selects <div id="parent">.

3

DOM Traversal Methods

Cause there's a train coming into the station
But it's heading for a new destination
                              — Devo,
          "It Doesn't Matter to Me"

In addition to the selector expressions described in Chapter 2, jQuery has a variety of DOM traversal methods to help us select elements in a document. These methods offer a great deal of flexibility, even allowing us to act upon multiple sets of elements in a single chain, like so:

```
$('div.section > p').addClass('lit').lt(1).addClass('profound');
```

At times the choice between a selector expression and a corresponding DOM traversal method is simply a matter of taste, but there is no doubt that the combined set of expressions and methods makes for an extremely powerful toolset for getting anything we want.

As of jQuery 1.1, DOM traversal methods do not modify the jQuery object they are sent to. Instead, a new jQuery object is constructed, which contains a reference to the original object. The original object can be retrieved with the .end method.

The jQuery Factory Function

The following function underpins the entire jQuery library as it allows us to create the jQuery objects that all of the other methods are attached to.

$()

> Creates a new jQuery object matching elements in the DOM.
> ```
> $(selector[, context])
> $(element)
> $(elementArray)
> $(object)
> $(html)
> ```

Parameters (first version)

- selector: A string containing a selector expression
- context (optional): The portion of the DOM tree within which to search

Parameters (second version)

- element: A DOM element to wrap in a jQuery object

Parameters (third version)

- elementArray: An array containing a set of DOM elements to wrap in a jQuery object

Parameters (fourth version)

- object: An existing jQuery object to clone

Parameters (fifth version)

- html: A string containing an HTML snippet describing new DOM elements to create

Return Value

The newly constructed jQuery object.

Description

In the first formulation listed above, $() searches through the DOM for any element that match the provided selector and creates a new jQuery object that references these elements:

```
$('div.foo');
```

In Chapter 2 we explored the range of selector expressions that can be used within this string.

Selector Context

By default, selectors perform their searches within the DOM starting at the document root. However, an alternative context can be given for the search by using the optional second parameter to the $() function. For example, if within a callback function we wish to do a search for an element, we can restrict that search:

```
$('div.foo').click(function() {
  $('span', this).addClass('bar');
});
```

Since we've restricted the span selector to the context of this, only spans within the clicked element will get the additional class.

Selector context is also useful for XML documents, as they do not form part of the default DOM tree. For example, if an AJAX call has returned an XML structure in the variable data, then we can perform searches within that structure:

```
$('//foo/bar', data)
```

Internally, selector context is implemented with the .find method, so $(selector, context) is equivalent to $(context).find(selector).

While the jQuery API only specifies DOM elements, arrays of DOM elements, and jQuery objects as valid contexts, in practice selectors and HTML snippets can be used here as well.

Wrapping DOM elements

The second and third formulations of this function allow us to create a jQuery object using a DOM element or elements that we have already found in some other way. A common use of this facility is to perform jQuery methods on an element that has been passed to a callback function in the keyword this:

```
$('div.foo').click(function() {
  $(this).slideUp();
});
```

This example causes elements to be hidden with a sliding animation when clicked. An element must be wrapped in a jQuery object before we call jQuery methods on it because the handler receives the clicked item in the keyword this as a bare DOM element.

Cloning jQuery Objects

When a jQuery object is passed as a parameter to the $ (), a new jQuery object is created that references the same DOM elements. The initial object can then be modified without affecting the new one.

Creating New Elements

If a string is passed as the parameter to $ (), jQuery examines the string to see if it looks like HTML. If not, the string is interpreted as a selector expression, as explained above. But if the string appears to be an HTML snippet, jQuery attempts to create new DOM elements as described by the HTML. Then a jQuery object is created and returned that refers to these elements. We can perform any of the usual jQuery methods on this object:

```
$('<p>My <em>new</em> paragraph</p>').appendTo('body');
```

The actual creation of the elements is handled by the browser's **innerHTML** mechanism. Specifically, jQuery creates a new <div> element and sets the innerHTML property of the element to the HTML snippet that was passed in. This means that to ensure cross-platform compatibility, the snippet must be well-formed. Tags that can contain other elements should always be paired with a closing tag:

```
$('<a></a>');
```

Tags that cannot contain elements should be quick-closed:

```
$('<img />');
```

Filtering Methods

These methods remove elements from the set matched by a jQuery object.

.filter()

> Reduces the set of matched elements to those that match the selector or pass the function's test.
>
>   .filter(selector)
>   .filter(function)

Parameters (first version)

- selector: A string containing a selector expression to match elements against

Parameters (second version)

- function: A function used as a test for each element in the set

Return Value

The new jQuery object.

Description

Given a jQuery object that represents a set of DOM elements, the `.filter` method constructs a new jQuery object from a subset of the matching elements. The supplied selector is tested against each element; all elements matching the selector will be included in the result.

Consider a page with a simple list on it:

```
<ul>
  <li>list item 1</li>
  <li>list item 2</li>
  <li>list item 3</li>
  <li>list item 4</li>
  <li>list item 5</li>
  <li>list item 6</li>
</ul>
```

We can apply this method to the set of list items:

```
$('li').filter(':even')
```

The result of this call is a jQuery object wrapping items 1, 3, and 5 as they match the selector (recall that :even and :odd use 0-based indexing).

Using a Filter Function

The second form of this method allows us to filter elements against a function rather than a selector. Suppose we have a more involved HTML snippet:

```
<ul>
  <li><strong>list</strong> item 1 - one strong</li>
  <li><strong>list</strong> item <strong>2</strong> - two
                                  <span>strongs</span></li>
  <li>list item 3</li>
  <li>list item 4</li>
  <li>list item 5</li>
  <li>list item 6</li>
</ul>
```

We can select the list items, and then filter them based on their contents:

```
$('li').filter(function(index) {
  return $("strong", this).length == 1;
})
```

The result of this expression will be the first list item only, as it contains exactly one `<strong>` tag. Within the filter function, `this` refers to each DOM element in turn. The parameter passed to the function tells us the index of that DOM element within the set matched by the jQuery object.

We can also take advantage of the `index` passed through the function:

```
$('li').filter(function(index) {
  return index % 3 == 2;
})
```

The result of this expression will be the third and sixth list items, as it uses the modulus operator (%) to select every item with an index value that, when divided by 3, has a remainder of 2.

.not()

Removes elements from the set of matched elements.

`.not(selector)`

`.not(elements)`

Parameters (first version)
- selector: A string containing a selector expression to match elements against

Parameters (second version)
- elements: One or more DOM elements to remove from the matched set

Return Value
The new jQuery object.

Description
Given a jQuery object that represents a set of DOM elements, the `.not` method constructs a new jQuery object from a subset of the matching elements. The supplied selector is tested against each element; the elements that don't match the selector will be included in the result.

Consider a page with a simple list on it:

```
<ul>
  <li>list item 1</li>
  <li>list item 2</li>
  <li>list item 3</li>
  <li>list item 4</li>
  <li>list item 5</li>
</ul>
```

We can apply this method to the set of list items:

```
$('li').not(':even')
```

The result of this call is a jQuery object wrapping items 2 and 4, as they do not match the selector (recall that :even and :odd use 0-based indexing).

Removing Specific Elements

The second version of the `.not` method allows us to remove elements from the matched set, assuming we have found those elements previously by some other means. For example, suppose our list had an identifier applied to one of its items:

```
<ul>
  <li>list item 1</li>
  <li>list item 2</li>
  <li id="notli">list item 3</li>
  <li>list item 4</li>
  <li>list item 5</li>
</ul>
```

We can fetch the third list item using the native JavaScript `getElementById` function, then remove it from a jQuery object:

```
$('li').not(document.getElementById('notli'))
```

This expression yields a jQuery object matching items 1, 2, 4, and 5. We could have accomplished the same thing with a simpler jQuery expression, but this technique can be useful when other libraries provide references to plain DOM nodes.

.contains()

Reduces the set of matched elements to those containing the specified text.

```
.contains(text)
```

Parameters
- text: A string of text to search for

Return Value
The new jQuery object.

Description
Given a jQuery object that represents a set of DOM elements, the `.contains` method constructs a new jQuery object from a subset of the matching elements. The supplied text is searched for in each element; all elements containing the text (even within a descendant element) will be included in the result.

Consider a page with a simple list on it:

```
<ul>
  <li>list item 1</li>
  <li>list <strong>item</strong> 2</li>
  <li>list item 3</li>
  <li>list item 4</li>
  <li>list item 5</li>
</ul>
```

We can apply this method to the set of list items:

```
$('li').contains('item 2')
```

The result of this call is a jQuery object wrapping item 2, as it contains the specified text. The search is performed using jQuery's `.text` method, so the search text can be located anywhere within the concatenation of the text strings in the matched set of elements or any of their descendants.

.eq()

> Reduces the set of matched elements to the one at the specified index.
>
> `.eq(index)`

Parameters
- index: An integer indicating the *0-based* position of the element

Return Value
The new jQuery object.

Description

Given a jQuery object that represents a set of DOM elements, the .eq method constructs a new jQuery object from one of the matching elements. The supplied index identifies the position of this element in the set.

Consider a page with a simple list on it:

```
<ul>
   <li>list item 1</li>
   <li>list item 2</li>
   <li>list item 3</li>
   <li>list item 4</li>
   <li>list item 5</li>
</ul>
```

We can apply this method to the set of list items:

```
$('li').eq(2)
```

The result of this call is a jQuery object wrapping item 3. Note that the supplied index is *0-based*, and refers to the position of the element within the jQuery object, *not* within the DOM tree.

.lt()

Reduces the set of matched elements to the ones before the specified index.

```
.lt(index)
```

Parameters

- index: An integer indicating the *0-based* position before which the elements are selected

Return Value

The new jQuery object.

Description

Given a jQuery object that represents a set of DOM elements, the .lt method constructs a new jQuery object from a subset of the matching elements. The supplied index identifies the position of one of the elements in the set; all elements before this one will be included in the result.

Consider a page with a simple list on it:

```
<ul>
  <li>list item 1</li>
  <li>list item 2</li>
  <li>list item 3</li>
  <li>list item 4</li>
  <li>list item 5</li>
</ul>
```

We can apply this method to the set of list items:

```
$('li').lt(2)
```

The result of this call is a jQuery object wrapping items 1 and 2. Note that the supplied index is *0-based*, and refers to the position of elements within the jQuery object, *not* within the DOM tree.

.gt()

Reduces the set of matched elements to the ones after the specified index.

`.gt(index)`

Parameters

- index: An integer indicating the *0-based* position after which the elements are selected

Return Value

The new jQuery object.

Description

Given a jQuery object that represents a set of DOM elements, the `.gt` method constructs a new jQuery object from a subset of the matching elements. The supplied `index` identifies the position of one of the elements in the set; all elements after this one will be included in the result.

Consider a page with a simple list on it:

```
<ul>
  <li>list item 1</li>
  <li>list item 2</li>
  <li>list item 3</li>
```

```
    <li>list item 4</li>
    <li>list item 5</li>
  </ul>
```

We can apply this method to the set of list items:

```
$('li').gt(2)
```

The result of this call is a jQuery object wrapping items 4 and 5. Note that the supplied index is *0-based*, and refers to the position of elements within the jQuery object, *not* within the DOM tree.

Tree Traversal Methods

These methods use the structure of the DOM tree to locate a new set of elements.

.find()

Gets the descendants of each element in the current set of matched elements, filtered by a selector.

```
.find(selector)
```

Parameters

• selector: A string containing a selector expression to match elements against

Return Value

The new jQuery object.

Description

Given a jQuery object that represents a set of DOM elements, the `.find` method allows us to search through the descendants of these elements in the DOM tree and construct a new jQuery object from the matching elements. The `.find` and `.children` methods are similar, except that the latter only travels a single level down the DOM tree.

The method accepts a selector expression of the same type that we can pass to the `$()` function. The elements will be filtered by testing whether they match this selector.

Consider a page with a basic nested list on it:

```
<ul class="level-1">
  <li class="item-i">I</li>
  <li class="item-ii">II
    <ul class="level-2">
      <li class="item-a">A</li>
      <li class="item-b">B
        <ul class="level-3">
          <li class="item-1">1</li>
          <li class="item-2">2</li>
          <li class="item-3">3</li>
        </ul>
      </li>
      <li class="item-c">C</li>
    </ul>
  </li>
  <li class="item-iii">III</li>
</ul>
```

If we begin at item II, we can find list items within it:

```
$('li.item-ii').find('li')
```

The result of this call is a jQuery object wrapping items A, B, 1, 2, 3, and C. Even though item II matches the selector expression, it is not included in the results; only descendants are considered candidates for the match.

As discussed in the section *The jQuery Factory Function*, selector context is implemented with the `.find` method; therefore, `$('li.item-ii').find('li')` is equivalent to `$('li', 'li.item-ii')`.

 Unlike in the rest of the tree traversal methods, the selector expression is required in a call to `.find()`. If we need to retrieve all of the descendant elements, we can pass in the selector * to accomplish this.

.children()

Gets children of each element in the set of matched elements, optionally filtered by a selector.

```
.children([selector])
```

Parameters

- selector (optional): A string containing a selector expression to match elements against

Return Value

The new jQuery object.

Description

Given a jQuery object that represents a set of DOM elements, the `.children` method allows us to search through the immediate children of these elements in the DOM tree and construct a new jQuery object from the matching elements. The `.find` and `.children` methods are similar, except that the latter only travels a single level down the DOM tree.

The method optionally accepts a selector expression of the same type that we can pass to the `$()` function. If the selector is supplied, the elements will be filtered by testing whether they match the selector.

Consider a page with a basic nested list on it:

```
<ul class="level-1">
  <li class="item-i">I</li>
  <li class="item-ii">II
    <ul class="level-2">
      <li class="item-a">A</li>
      <li class="item-b">B
        <ul class="level-3">
          <li class="item-1">1</li>
          <li class="item-2">2</li>
          <li class="item-3">3</li>
        </ul>
      </li>
      <li class="item-c">C</li>
    </ul>
  </li>
  <li class="item-iii">III</li>
</ul>
```

If we begin at the level-2 list, we can find its children:

```
$('ul.level-2').children()
```

The result of this call is a jQuery object wrapping items A, B, and C. Since we do not supply a selector expression, all of the children are part of the object. If we had supplied one, only the matching items among these three would be included.

.parents()

Gets the ancestors of each element in the current set of matched elements, optionally filtered by a selector.

```
.parents([selector])
```

Parameters

- selector (optional): A string containing a selector expression to match elements against

Return Value

The new jQuery object.

Description

Given a jQuery object that represents a set of DOM elements, the .parents method allows us to search through the ancestors of these elements in the DOM tree and construct a new jQuery object from the matching elements. The .parents() and .parent() methods are similar, except that the latter only travels a single level up the DOM tree.

The method optionally accepts a selector expression of the same type that we can pass to the $() function. If the selector is supplied, the elements will be filtered by testing whether they match the selector.

Consider a page with a basic nested list on it:

```
<ul class="level-1">
  <li class="item-i">I</li>
  <li class="item-ii">II
    <ul class="level-2">
      <li class="item-a">A</li>
      <li class="item-b">B
        <ul class="level-3">
          <li class="item-1">1</li>
          <li class="item-2">2</li>
          <li class="item-3">3</li>
        </ul>
      </li>
      <li class="item-c">C</li>
    </ul>
  </li>
  <li class="item-iii">III</li>
</ul>
```

If we begin at item A, we can find its ancestors:

```
$('li.item-a').parents()
```

The result of this call is a jQuery object wrapping the `level-2` list, `item ii`, and the `level-1` list (and on up the DOM tree all the way to the `<html>` element). Since we do not supply a selector expression, all of the ancestors are part of the object. If we had supplied one, only the matching items among these would be included.

.parent()

Gets the parent of each element in the current set of matched elements, optionally filtered by a selector.

```
.parent([selector])
```

Parameters

- selector (optional): A string containing a selector expression to match elements against.

Return Value

The new jQuery object.

Description

Given a jQuery object that represents a set of DOM elements, the `.parent` method allows us to search through the parents of these elements in the DOM tree and construct a new jQuery object from the matching elements. The `.parents` and `.parent` methods are similar, except that the latter only travels a single level up the DOM tree.

The method optionally accepts a selector expression of the same type that we can pass to the `$()` function. If the selector is supplied, the elements will be filtered by testing whether they match the selector.

Consider a page with a basic nested list on it:

```
<ul class="level-1">
  <li class="item-i">I</li>
  <li class="item-ii">II
    <ul class="level-2">
      <li class="item-a">A</li>
      <li class="item-b">B
        <ul class="level-3">
```

```
            <li class="item-1">1</li>
            <li class="item-2">2</li>
            <li class="item-3">3</li>
          </ul>
        </li>
        <li class="item-c">C</li>
      </ul>
    </li>
    <li class="item-iii">III</li>
  </ul>
```

If we begin at item A, we can find its parents:

```
$('li.item-a').parent()
```

The result of this call is a jQuery object wrapping the `level-2` list. Since we do not supply a selector expression, the parent element is unequivocally included as part of the object. If we had supplied one, the element would be tested for a match before it was included.

.siblings()

> Gets the siblings of each element in the set of matched elements, optionally filtered by a selector.
>
> ```
> .siblings([selector])
> ```

Parameters

- selector (optional): A string containing a selector expression to match elements against

Return Value

The new jQuery object.

Description

Given a jQuery object that represents a set of DOM elements, the `.siblings` method allows us to search through the siblings of these elements in the DOM tree and construct a new jQuery object from the matching elements.

The method optionally accepts a selector expression of the same type that we can pass to the `$()` function. If the selector is supplied, the elements will be filtered by testing whether they match the selector.

Consider a page with a simple list on it:

```
<ul>
    <li>list item 1</li>
    <li>list item 2</li>
    <li class="third-item">list item 3</li>
    <li>list item 4</li>
    <li>list item 5</li>
</ul>
```

If we begin at the third item, we can find its siblings:

```
$('li.third-item').siblings()
```

The result of this call is a jQuery object wrapping items 1, 2, 4, and 5. Since we do not supply a selector expression, all of the siblings are part of the object. If we had supplied one, only the matching items among these four would be included.

The original element is not included among the siblings, which is important to remember when we wish to find all elements at a particular level of the DOM tree.

.prev()

Gets the immediately preceding sibling of each element in the set of matched elements, optionally filtered by a selector.

```
.prev([selector])
```

Parameters

- selector (optional): A string containing a selector expression to match against the elements

Return Value

The new jQuery object.

Description

Given a jQuery object that represents a set of DOM elements, the .prev method allows us to search through the predecessors of these elements in the DOM tree and construct a new jQuery object from the matching elements.

The method optionally accepts a selector expression of the same type that we can pass to the $() function. If the selector is supplied, the elements will be filtered by testing whether they match the selector.

Consider a page with a simple list on it:

```
<ul>
    <li>list item 1</li>
    <li>list item 2</li>
    <li class="third-item">list item 3</li>
    <li>list item 4</li>
    <li>list item 5</li>
</ul>
```

If we begin at the third item, we can find the element that comes just before it:

```
$('li.third-item').prev()
```

The result of this call is a jQuery object wrapping item 2. Since we do not supply a selector expression, this preceding element is unequivocally included as part of the object. If we had supplied one, the element would be tested for a match before it was included.

.next()

Gets the immediately following sibling of each element in the set of matched elements, optionally filtered by a selector.

```
.next([selector])
```

Parameters

- selector (optional): A string containing a selector expression to match against the elements

Return Value

The new jQuery object.

Description

Given a jQuery object that represents a set of DOM elements, the .next method allows us to search through the successors of these elements in the DOM tree and construct a new jQuery object from the matching elements.

The method optionally accepts a selector expression of the same type that we can pass to the $() function. If the selector is supplied, the elements will be filtered by testing whether they match the selector.

Consider a page with a simple list on it:

```
<ul>
    <li>list item 1</li>
    <li>list item 2</li>
    <li class="third-item">list item 3</li>
    <li>list item 4</li>
    <li>list item 5</li>
</ul>
```

If we begin at the third item, we can find the element that comes just after it:

```
$('li.third-item').next()
```

The result of this call is a jQuery object wrapping item 4. Since we do not supply a selector expression, this following element is unequivocally included as part of the object. If we had supplied one, the element would be tested for a match before it was included.

Miscellaneous Traversal Methods

These methods provide other mechanisms for manipulating the set of matched DOM elements in a jQuery object.

.add()

Adds elements to the set of matched elements.

    `.add(selector)`

    `.add(elements)`

    `.add(html)`

Parameters (first version)

- selector: A string containing a selector expression to match additional elements against

Parameters (second version)

- elements: one or more elements to add to the set of matched elements

Parameters (third version)

- html: An HTML fragment to add to the set of matched elements

Return Value

The new jQuery object.

Description

Given a jQuery object that represents a set of DOM elements, the `.add` method constructs a new jQuery object from the union of those elements and the ones passed into the method. The argument to `.add` can be pretty much anything that `$()` accepts, including a jQuery selector expression, references to DOM elements, or an HTML snippet.

Consider a page with a simple list and a paragraph following it:

```
<ul>
  <li>list item 1</li>
  <li>list item 2</li>
  <li>list item 3</li>
</ul>
<p>a paragraph</p>
```

We can select the list items and then the paragraph by using either a selector or a reference to the DOM element itself as the `.add` method's argument:

```
$('li').add('p')  or
$('li').add(document.getElementsByTagName('p')[0])
```

The result of this call is a jQuery object wrapping all four elements.

Using an HTML snippet as the `.add` method's argument (as in the third version) we can create additional elements on the fly and add those elements to the matched set of elements. Let's say, for example, that we want to add a class `foo` to the list items, the paragraph, and a newly created paragraph:

```
$('li').add('p').add('<p id="new">new paragraph</p>').addClass('foo')
```

Although the new paragraph has been created and its `foo` class added, it still does not appear on the page. To place it on the page, we can add one of the insertion methods to the chain.

For more information about the insertion methods please refer to Chapter 4.

.is()

Checks the current matched set of elements against a selector and returns `true` if at least one of these elements matches the selector.

```
.is(selector)
```

Parameters

- selector: A string containing a selector expression to match elements against

Return Value

A boolean indicating whether an element matches the selector.

Description

Unlike the rest of the methods in this chapter, `.is()` does not create a new jQuery object. Instead, it allows us to test the contents of a jQuery object without modification. This is often useful in callbacks, such as event handlers.

Suppose we have a list, with two of its items containing a child element:

```
<ul>
  <li>list <strong>item 1</strong></li>
  <li><span>list item 2</span></li>
  <li>list item 3</li>
</ul>
```

We can attach a click handler to the `<ul>` element, and then limit the code to be triggered only when a list item itself, not one of its children, is clicked:

```
$('ul').click(function(event) {
  if ($(event.target).is('li') ) {
    $(event.target).remove();
  }
});
```

Now, when the user clicks on the word `list` in the first item or anywhere in the third item, the clicked list item will be removed from the document. However, when the user clicks on `item 1` in the first item or anywhere in the second item, nothing will occur, because for those target of the event would be `<strong>` and `<span>` respectively.

.end()

Ends the most recent filtering operation in the current chain and returns the set of matched elements to its previous state.

```
.end()
```

Parameters

None.

Return Value

The previous jQuery object.

Description

Most of the methods in this chapter operate on a jQuery object and produce a new one, matching a different set of DOM elements. When this happens, it is as if a new set of elements is pushed onto a stack that is maintained inside the object. Each successive filtering method pushed a new element set onto the stack. If we need an older element set, we can use .end() to pop the sets back off of the stack.

Suppose we have a couple of short lists on a page:

```
<ul class="first">
    <li class="foo">list item 1</li>
    <li>list item 2</li>
    <li class="bar">list item 3</li>
</ul>
<ul class="second">
    <li class="foo">list item 1</li>
    <li>list item 2</li>
    <li class="bar">list item 3</li>
</ul>
```

The .end method is useful primarily when exploiting jQuery's chaining properties. When not using chaining, we can usually just call up a previous object by variable name, so that we don't need to manipulate the stack. With .end(), though, we can string all the method calls together:

```
$('ul.first').find('.foo').addClass('some-class').end()
                        .find('.bar').addClass('another-class');
```

This chain searches for items with the class `foo` within the first list only and adds the class `some-class` to them. Then `.end()` returns the object to its state before the call to `.find()`, so the second `.find()` looks for `.bar` inside `<ul class="first">`, not just inside that list's `<li class="foo">`, and adds the class `another-class` to the matching element. The result is that items 1 and 3 of the first list have a class added to them, and none of the items from the second list do.

A long jQuery chain can be visualized as a structured code block, with filtering methods providing the openings of nested blocks and `.end` methods closing them:

```
$('#example-traversing-end ul.first').find('.foo')
  .addClass('some-class')
    .end()
      .find('.bar')
        .addClass('another-class');
  .end();
```

The last `.end()` is unnecessary, as we are discarding the jQuery object immediately thereafter. However, when the code is written in this form the `.end()` provides visual symmetry and closure—making the program, at least to the eyes of some developers, more readable.

4

DOM Manipulation Methods

Washed his hands of a deadly fate
He put himself in an altered state
> *— Devo,*
> *"Mecha-mania Boy"*

All of the methods in this chapter manipulate the DOM in some manner. A few of them simply change one of the attributes of an element, while others set an element's style properties. Still others modify entire elements (or groups of elements) themselves — inserting, copying, removing, and so on.

A few of these methods such as `.attr()`, `.html()`, and `.val()` also act as **getters**, retrieving information from DOM elements for later use.

General Attributes

.attr(attribute)

> Gets the value of an attribute for the first element in the set of matched elements.
>
> ```
> .attr(attribute)
> ```

Parameters

- attribute: The name of the attribute to get

Return Value

A string containing the attribute value.

Description

We can get any attribute of an element rather easily without jQuery, by using the native JavaScript function `getAttribute`. Additionally, most of these attributes are available through JavaScript as DOM node properties. Some of the more common properties are:

- `className`
- `tagName`
- `id`
- `href`
- `title`
- `rel`
- `src`

Let's consider the following link:

```
<a id="myid" href="/archives/jquery-links.htm" title="A few jQuery
                            links from long ago">old jQuery links</a>
```

Using jQuery's `.attr` method to get an element's attribute has two main advantages:

1. **Convenience**: it can be chained to a jQuery object.
2. **Cross-browser consistency**: The `.attr` method always gets the actual attribute text, regardless of which browser is being used. On the other hand, when using `getAttribute()` with attributes such as `href`, `src`, and `cite`, some browsers (correctly) get the attribute text, while others get the absolute URL, regardless of whether the attribute has an absolute URL or a relative one.

In order to use `getAttribute()` or any of an element's properties as a substitute for `.attr()`, we need to make sure that we are working with a DOM node rather than a jQuery object. To convert the first element represented in a jQuery object to a DOM node, we can use either `[0]` or `.get(0)`.

All of the following use `getAttribute('title')` to get its `title` attribute:

1. `document.getElementById('myid').getAttribute('title')`
2. `$('#myid').get(0).getAttribute('title')`
3. `$('#myid')[0].getAttribute('title')`

With any of these options, we could replace `.getAttribute('title')` with `.title`.

.attr()

Sets one or more attributes for the set of matched elements.

    .attr(attribute, value)

    .attr(map)

    .attr(attribute, function)

Parameters (first version)

- attribute: The name of the attribute to set
- value: A value to set for the attribute

Parameters (second version)

- map: A map of attribute-value pairs to set

Parameters (third version)

- attribute: The name of the attribute to set
- function: A function returning the value to set

Return Value

The jQuery object, for chaining purposes.

Description

The .attr method is a convenient and powerful way to set the value of attributes especially when setting multiple attributes or values returned by a function. Let's consider the following image:

```
<img id="greatphoto" src="brush-seller.jpg" alt="brush seller" />
```

.attr(attribute, value)

We change the alt attribute by putting 'alt' followed by a comma and the new value inside the .attr method's parentheses:

```
$('#greatphoto').attr('alt', 'Beijing Brush Seller');
```

We can *add* an attribute in the same way:

```
$('#greatphoto').attr('title', 'Beijing Brush Seller - photo
                                    by Kelly Clark');
```

.attr({map})

To change the `alt` attribute and add the `title` attribute at the same time, we can pass both sets of names and values into the method at once using a map (JavaScript object syntax). We join each attribute to its value with a colon and separate each pair with a comma:

```
$('#greatphoto').attr({alt:'Beijing Brush Seller', title:
                    'Beijing Brush Seller - photo by Kelly Clark'});
```

When setting multiple attributes, the quotation marks around the attribute names are optional.

.attr(attribute, function)

By using a function to set attributes, we can concatenate a new value with an existing value:

```
$('#greatphoto').attr({alt: function() {return 'Beijing ' +
            this.alt}, title: function() {return 'Beijing ' +
                    this.alt + ' - photo by Kelly Clark'}});
```

This use of a function can be even more useful when we apply the attributes to multiple elements.

.removeAttr()

Removes an attribute from each element in the set of matched elements.

```
.removeAttr(attribute)
```

Parameters

- attribute: An attribute

Return Value

The jQuery object, for chaining purposes.

Description

The `.removeAttr` method uses the JavaScript `removeAttribute` function, but it has the advantage of being able to be chained to a jQuery selector expression.

Style Properties

.css(property)

> Gets the value of a style property for the first element in the set of matched elements.
>
>   .css(property)

Parameters

- property: A CSS property

Return Value

A string containing the CSS property value.

Description

The .css method is a convenient way to get a style property from the first matched element, especially in the light of the different terms browser's use for certain properties. For example, Internet Explorer's DOM implementation refers to the float property as styleFloat, while Mozilla-based browsers refer to it as cssFloat. The .css method accounts for such differences, producing the same result no matter which term we use. For example, an element that is floated left will return the string left for each of the following three lines:

1. `$('div.left').css('float');`
2. `$('div.left').css('cssFloat');`
3. `$('div.left').css('styleFloat');`

Also, jQuery can equally interpret the CSS and DOM formatting of multiple-word properties. For example, jQuery understands and returns the correct value for both .css('background-color') and .css('backgroundColor').

.css()

Sets one or more CSS properties for the set of matched elements.

```
.css(property, value)
.css(map)
.css(property, function)
```

Parameters (first version)
- property: A CSS property name
- value: A value to set for the property

Parameters (second version)
- map: A map of property-value pairs to set

Parameters (third version)
- property: A CSS property name
- function: A function returning the value to set

Return Value

The jQuery object, for chaining purposes.

Description

As with the `.attr` method, the `.css` method makes setting properties of elements quick and easy. This method can take either a comma-separated key-value pair or a map of colon-separated key-value pairs (JavaScript object notation).

Also, jQuery can equally interpret the CSS and DOM formatting of multiple-word properties. For example, jQuery understands and returns the correct value for both `.css({'background-color':'#ffe', 'border-left': '5px solid #ccc'})` and `.css({backgroundColor:'#ffe', borderLeft: '5px solid #ccc'})`. Notice that with the DOM notation, quotation marks around the property names are optional, but with CSS notation they're required due to the hyphen in the name.

Since the `.css` method calls the `.attr` method internally, we can also pass a function as the property value:

```
$('div.example').css('width', function(index) {
  return index * 50;
});
```

This example sets the widths of the matched elements to incrementally larger values.

.height()

> Gets the current computed height for the first element in the set of matched elements.
>
>   .height()

Parameters

None.

Return Value

The height of the element, in pixels.

Description

The difference between `.css('height')` and `.height()` is that the latter returns a unit-less pixel value (for example, `400`) while the former returns a value with units intact (for example, `400px`). The `.height` method is recommended when an element's height needs to be used in a mathematical calculation.

.height(value)

> Sets the CSS height of each element in the set of matched elements.
>
>   .height(value)

Parameters

- value: An integer representing the number of pixels, or an integer with an optional unit of measure appended

Return Value

The jQuery object, for chaining purposes.

Description

With `.height('value')`, unlike with `.css('height','value')`, the value can be either a string (number and unit) or a number. If only a number is provided for the value, jQuery assumes a pixel unit.

.width()

> Gets the current computed width for the first element in the set of matched elements.
>
> `.width()`

Parameters

None.

Return Value

The width of the element, in pixels.

Description

The difference between `.css(width)` and `.width()` is that the latter returns a unit-less pixel value (for example, `400`) while the former returns a value with units intact (for example, `400px`). The `.width` method is recommended when an element's width needs to be used in a mathematical calculation.

.width(value)

> Sets the CSS width of each element in the set of matched elements.
>
> `.width(value)`

Parameters

- value: An integer representing the number of pixels, or an integer along with an optional unit of measure appended

Return Value

The jQuery object, for chaining purposes.

Description

With `.width('value')`, unlike with `.css('width', 'value')`, the value can be either a string (number and unit) or a number. If only a number is provided for the value, jQuery assumes a pixel unit.

Class Attribute

.addClass()

> Adds one or more classes to each element in the set of matched elements.
>
> ```
> .addClass(class)
> ```

Parameters

- class: One or more class names to be added to the class attribute of each matched element

Return Value

The jQuery object, for chaining purposes.

Description

It's important to note that this method does *not* replace a class; it simply *adds* the class.

More than one class may be added at a time, separated by a space, to the set of matched elements, like so: $('p').addClass('myclass yourclass').

This method is often used with .removeClass() to switch elements' classes from one to another, like so:

```
$('p').removeClass('myclass noclass').addClass('yourclass')
```

Here, the myclass and noclass classes are removed from all paragraphs, while yourclass is added.

.removeClass()

> Removes one or all classes from each element in the set of matched elements.
>
> ```
> .removeClass([class])
> ```

Parameters

- class (optional): A class name to be removed from the class attribute of each matched element

Return Value

The jQuery object, for chaining purposes.

Description

If a class name is included as a parameter, then only that class will be removed from the set of matched elements. If no class names are specified in the parameter, all classes will be removed.

More than one class may be removed at a time, separated by a space, from the set of matched elements, like so: `$('p').removeClass('myclass yourclass')`.

This method is often used with `.addClass()` to switch elements' classes from one to another, like so:

```
$('p').removeClass('myclass').addClass('yourclass')
```

Here, the class `myclass` is removed from all the paragraphs, while `yourclass` is added.

To replace all existing classes with another class, use `.attr('class','new-class')` instead.

.toggleClass()

> If the class is present, `.toggleClass()` removes it from each element in the set of matched elements; if it is not present, it adds the class.
>
> ```
> .toggleClass(class)
> ```

Parameters

- class: A class name to be toggled in the class attribute of each element in the matched set

Return Value

The jQuery object, for chaining purposes.

Description

This method takes one or more class names as its parameter. If an element in the matched set of elements already has the class, then it is removed; if an element does not have the class, then it is added. For example, we can apply `.toggleClass()` to a simple `<div>`:

```
<div class="tumble">Some text.</div>
```

The first time we apply `$('div.tumble').toggleClass('bounce')`, we get the following:

```
<div class="tumble bounce">Some text.</div>
```

The second time we apply `$('div.tumble').toggleClass('bounce')`, the `<div>` class is returned to the single `tumble` value:

```
<div class="tumble">Some text.</div>
```

Applying `.toggleClass('bounce spin')` to the same `<div>` alternates between `<div class="tumble bounce spin'>` and `<div class="tumble'>`.

DOM Replacement

.html()

Gets the HTML contents of the first element in the set of matched elements.

```
.html()
```

Parameters
None.

Return Value
A string containing the HTML representation of the element.

Description
This method is not available on XML documents.

In an HTML document, we can use the `.html` method to get the contents of any element. If our selector expression matches more than one element, only the first one's HTML content is returned. Consider this code:

```
$('div.demo-container').html();
```

In order for the following `<div>` tag's content to be retrieved, it would have to be the first one in the document:

```
<div class="demo-container">
  <div class="demo-box">Demonstration Box
  </div>
</div>
```

The result would look like this:

```
<div class="demo-box">Demonstration Box</div>
```

.html(HTML)

Sets the HTML contents of each element in the set of matched elements.
```
.html(HTML)
```

Parameters

- HTML: A string of HTML to set as the content of each matched element

Return Value

The jQuery object, for chaining purposes.

Description

The .html(HTML) is not available in XML documents.

When we use .html(HTML) to set elements' contents, any contents that were in those elements is completely replaced by the new contents. Consider the following HTML:

```
<div class="demo-container">
  <div class="demo-box">Demonstration Box
  </div>
</div>
```

We can set the HTML contents of <div class="demo-container"> like so:

```
$('div.demo-container').html('<p>All new content.
                                      <em>You bet!</em>');
```

That line of code will replace everything inside <div class="demo-container">:

```
<div class="demo-container"><p>All new content.
                                      <em>You bet!</em></div>
```

.text()

Gets the combined text contents of each element in the set of matched elements, including their descendants.
```
.text()
```

Parameters

None.

Return Value

A string containing the combined text contents of the matched elements.

Description

Unlike the .html method, the .text method can be used in both XML and HTML documents. The result of the .text method is a string containing the combined text of all matched elements. Consider the following HTML:

```
<div class="demo-container">
  <div class="demo-box">Demonstration Box
  </div>
  <ul>
    <li>list item 1</li>
    <li>list <strong>item</strong> 2</li>
  </ul>
</div>
```

The code $('div.demo-container').text() would produce the following result:

```
Demonstration Boxlist item 1list item 2
```

.text(text)

> Sets the content of each element in the set of matched elements to the specified text.
>
> ```
> .text(text)
> ```

Parameters

- text: A string of text to set as the content of each matched element

Return Value

The jQuery object, for chaining purposes.

Description

Unlike the .html(html) method, .text(text) can be used in both XML and HTML documents.

We need to be aware that this method replaces < and > with < and >, respectively. Consider the following HTML:

```
<div class="demo-container">
  <div class="demo-box">Demonstration Box
  </div>
  <ul>
    <li>list item 1</li>
    <li>list <strong>item</strong> 2</li>
  </ul>
</div>
```

The code $('div.demo-container').text('<p>This is a test.</p>') will produce the following HTML:

```
<div class="demo-container">&lt;p&gt;This is a test.&lt;/p&gt;</div>
```

It will appear on a rendered page as though the tags were exposed, like this:

```
<p>This is a test</p>
```

.val()

> Gets the current value of the first element in the set of matched elements.
>
> ```
> .val()
> ```

Parameters
None.

Return Value
A string containing the value of the element.

Description
The .val method is primarily used to get the value of form elements.

.val(value)

> Sets the value of each element in the set of matched elements.
>
> ```
> .val(value)
> ```

Parameters

- value: A string of text to set as the value property of each matched element

Return Value

The jQuery object, for chaining purposes.

Description

This method is typically used to set the value of form fields.

DOM Insertion, Inside

.prepend()

Inserts content, specified by the parameter, at the beginning of each element in the set of matched elements.

```
.prepend(content)
```

Parameters

- content: An element, HTML string, or jQuery object to insert at the beginning of each element in the set of matched elements

Return Value

The jQuery object, for chaining purposes.

Description

The .prepend and .prependTo methods perform the same task. The only difference is in the syntax—specifically, in the placement of the content and target. With .prepend(), the selector expression preceding the method is the container into which the content is inserted. With .prependTo(), on the other hand, the *content* precedes the method, either as a selector expression or as markup created on the fly, and it is inserted into the target container.

Consider the following HTML:

```
<div class="demo-container">
  <div class="demo-box">Demonstration Box
  </div>
</div>
```

The two `<div>`s, with a little CSS, are rendered on the right side of the page as follows:

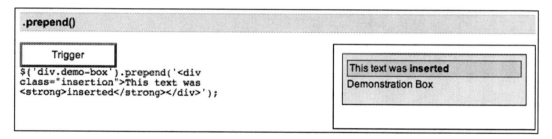

We can insert an HTML structure into the beginning of `<div class="demo-box">` like so:

```
$('div.demo-box').prepend('<div class="insertion">This text was
                                    <strong>inserted</strong></div>');
```

The new `<div>` and `<strong>` elements as well as the text nodes are created on the fly and added to the DOM. The result is a new `<div>` positioned just before the **Demonstration Box** text:

An element (or array of elements) that already exists on the page could be moved to the beginning of `<div class="demo-box">` as well. The following code, for example, moves the document's first paragraph by using a jQuery object:

```
$('div.demo-box').prepend( $('p:eq(0)') );
```

.prependTo()

Inserts every element in the set of matched elements at the beginning of the target.

```
.prependTo(target)
```

Parameters

- target: A selector, element, HTML string, or jQuery object; the matched set of elements will be inserted at the beginning of the element(s) specified by this parameter

Return Value

The jQuery object, for chaining purposes.

Description

The .prepend and .prependTo methods perform the same task. The only difference is in the syntax—specifically, in the placement of the content and target. With .prepend(), the selector expression preceding the method is the container into which the content is inserted. With .prependTo(), on the other hand, the *content* precedes the method, either as a selector expression or as markup created on the fly, and it is inserted into the target container.

Consider the following HTML:

```
<div class="demo-container">
   <div class="demo-box">Demonstration Box
   </div>
</div>
```

The two <div>s, with a little CSS, are rendered on the right side of the page as follows:

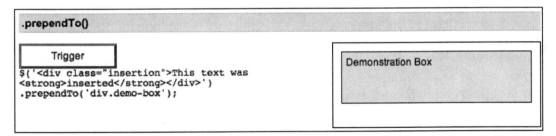

Using .prependTo(), we can insert an HTML structure into the beginning of <div class="demo-box"> like so.

```
$('<div class="insertion">This text was <strong>inserted</strong>
                        </div>').prependTo('div.demo-box');
```

The new `<div>` and `<strong>` elements, as well as the text nodes, are created on the fly and added to the DOM. The result is a new `<div>` positioned just before the **Demonstration Box** text:

```
.prependTo()

┌─────────────┐
│   Trigger   │
└─────────────┘
$('<div class="insertion">This text was
<strong>inserted</strong></div>')
.prependTo('div.demo-box');
```

```
This text was inserted
Demonstration Box
```

An element (or array of elements) that already exists on the page could be moved to the beginning of `<div class="demo-box">` as well. The following code, for example, moves the document's first paragraph by using a selector expression both for the content to be inserted and for the target:

```
$('p:eq(0)').prependTo('div.demo-box');
```

.append()

Inserts content specified by the parameter at the end of each element in the set of matched elements.

```
.append(content)
```

Parameters

- content: A selector, element, HTML string, or jQuery object to insert at the end of each element in the set of matched elements.

Return Value

The jQuery object, for chaining purposes.

Description

The .append and .appendTo methods perform the same task. The only difference is in the syntax — specifically, in the placement of the content and target. With .append(), the selector expression preceding the method is the container into which the content is inserted. With .appendTo(), on the other hand, the *content* precedes the method, either as a selector expression or as markup created on the fly, and it is inserted into the target container.

Consider the following HTML:

```
<div class="demo-container">
  <div class="demo-box">Demonstration Box
  </div>
</div>
```

The two `<div>`s, with a little CSS, are rendered on the right side of the page as follows:

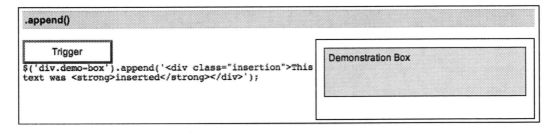

We can insert an HTML structure into the end of `<div class="demo-box">` like so:

```
$('div.demo-box').append('<div class="insertion">This text
                         was <strong>inserted</strong></div>');
```

The new `<div>` and `<strong>` elements, as well as the text nodes, are created on the fly and added to the DOM. The result is a new `<div>` positioned just after the **Demonstration Box** text:

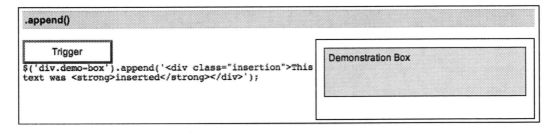

An element (or array of elements) that already exists on the page could be moved to the end of `<div class="demo-box">` as well. The following code, for example, moves the document's first paragraph by using a jQuery object:

```
$('div.demo-box').append( $('p:eq(0)') );
```

.appendTo()

Inserts every element in the set of matched elements at the end of the target.

    `.appendTo(target)`

Parameters

- target: A selector, element, HTML string, or jQuery object; the matched set of elements will be inserted at the end of the element(s) specified by this parameter

Return Value

The jQuery object, for chaining purposes.

Description

The `.append` and `.appendTo` methods perform the same task. The only difference is in the syntax—specifically, in the placement of the content and target. With `.append()`, the selector expression preceding the method is the container into which the content is inserted. With `.appendTo()`, on the other hand, the *content* precedes the method, either as a selector expression or as markup created on the fly, and it is inserted into the target container.

Consider the following HTML:

```
<div class="demo-container">
  <div class="demo-box">Demonstration Box
  </div>
</div>
```

The two `<div>`s, with a little CSS, are rendered on the right side of the page as follows:

.appendTo()

    Trigger

```
$('<div class="insertion">This text was
<strong>inserted</strong></div>')
.appendTo('div.demo-box');
```

Demonstration Box

Using `.appendTo()`, we can insert an HTML structure into the end of `<div class="demo-box">` like so:

```
$('<div class="insertion">This text was <strong>inserted</strong>
                                    </div>').appendTo('div.demo-box');
```

The new `<div>` and `<strong>` elements, as well as the text nodes, are created on the fly and added to the DOM. The result is a new `<div>` positioned just after the **Demonstration Box** text:

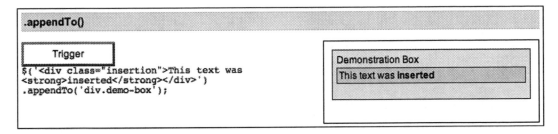

An element (or array of elements) that already exists on the page could be moved to the end of `<div class="demo-box">` as well. The following code, for example, moves the document's first paragraph by using a selector expression both for the content to be inserted and for the target:

```
$('p:eq(0)').appendTo('div.demo-box');
```

DOM Insertion, Outside

.before()

Inserts content specified by the parameter before each element in the set of matched elements.

```
.before(content)
```

Parameters

- content: An element, HTML string, or jQuery object to insert before each element in the set of matched elements

Return Value

The jQuery object, for chaining purposes.

Description

The `.before` and `.insertBefore` methods perform the same task. The only difference is in the syntax — specifically, in the placement of the content and target. With `.before()`, the selector expression preceding the method is the container into which the content is inserted. With `.insertBefore()`, on the other hand, the *content* precedes the method, either as a selector expression or as markup created on the fly, and it is inserted before the target container.

Consider the following HTML:

```
<div class="demo-container">
  <div class="demo-box">Demonstration Box
  </div>
</div>
```

The two `<div>`s, with a little CSS, are rendered on the right side of the page as follows:

We can insert an HTML structure before `<div class="demo-box">` like so:

```
$('div.demo-box').before('<div class="insertion">This text
                          was <strong>inserted</strong></div>');
```

The new `<div>` and `<strong>` elements, as well as the text nodes, are created on the fly and added to the DOM. The result is a new `<div>` positioned outside of, just before, `<div class="demo-box">`:

An element (or array of elements) that already exists on the page could be moved to the DOM position just before `<div class="demo-box">` as well. The following code, for example, moves the document's first paragraph by using a jQuery object:

```
$('div.demo-box').before( $('p:eq(0)') );
```

.insertBefore()

> Inserts every element in the set of matched elements before the set of elements specified in the parameter.
>
> `.insertBefore(content)`

Parameters

- content: A selector or element before which the matched set of elements will be inserted

Return Value

The jQuery object, for chaining purposes.

Description

The `.before` and `.insertBefore` methods perform the same task. The only difference is in the syntax—specifically, in the placement of the content and target. With `.before()`, the selector expression preceding the method is the container into which the content is inserted. With `.insertBefore()`, on the other hand, the *content* precedes the method, either as a selector expression or as markup created on the fly, and it is inserted before the target container.

Consider the following HTML:

```
<div class="demo-container">
  <div class="demo-box">Demonstration Box
  </div>
</div>
```

The two <div>s, with a little CSS, are rendered on the right side of the page as follows:

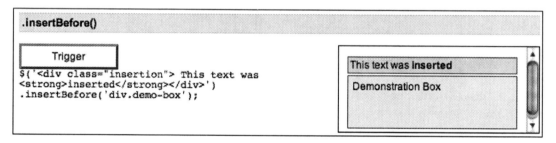

We can insert an HTML structure just before <div class="demo-box"> like so:

```
$('<div class="insertion">This text was <strong>inserted</strong>
                              </div>').insertBefore('div.demo-box');
```

The new <div> and <strong> elements, as well as the text nodes, are created on the fly and added to the DOM. The result is a new <div> positioned outside of, just before, <div class="demo-box">:

An element (or array of elements) that already exists on the page could be moved to the DOM position just before <div class="demo-box"> as well. The following code, for example, moves the document's first paragraph by using a jQuery object:

```
$('p:eq(0)').insertBefore('div.demo-box');
```

.after()

Inserts content specified by the parameter after each element in the set of matched elements.

```
.after(content)
```

Parameters

- content: An element, HTML string, or jQuery object to insert after each element in the set of matched elements.

Return Value

The jQuery object, for chaining purposes.

Description

The .after and .insertAfter methods perform the same task. The only difference is in the syntax—specifically, in the placement of the content and target. With .after(), the selector expression preceding the method is the container after which the content is inserted. With .insertAfter(), on the other hand, the *content* precedes the method, either as a selector expression or as markup created on the fly, and it is inserted after the target container.

Consider the following HTML:

```
<div class="demo-container">
  <div class="demo-box">Demonstration Box
  </div>
</div>
```

The two <div>s, with a little CSS, are rendered on the right side of the page as follows:

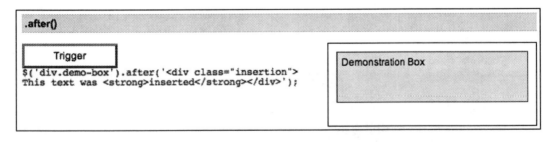

We can insert an HTML structure after <div class="demo-box"> like so:

```
$('div.demo-box').after('<div class="insertion">This text
                        was <strong>inserted</strong></div>');
```

The new `<div>` and `<strong>` elements, as well as the text nodes, are created on the fly and added to the DOM. The result is a new `<div>` positioned outside of, just after, `<div class="demo-box">`:

```
.after()

   Trigger
${'div.demo-box'}.after('<div class="insertion">
This text was <strong>inserted</strong></div>');
```

Demonstration Box

This text was **inserted**

An element (or array of elements) that already exists on the page could be moved to the DOM position just after `<div class="demo-box">` as well. The following code, for example, moves the document's first paragraph by using a jQuery object:

```
$('div.demo-box').after( $('p:eq(0)') );
```

.insertAfter()

> Inserts every element in the set of matched elements after the set of elements specified in the parameter.
>
>   .insertAfter(content)

Parameters

- content: A selector or element after which the matched set of elements will be inserted

Return Value

The jQuery object, for chaining purposes.

Description

The `.after` and `.insertAfter` methods perform the same task. The only difference is in the syntax—specifically, in the placement of the content and target. With `.after()`, the selector expression preceding the method is the container after which the content is inserted. With `.insertAfter()`, on the other hand, the *content* precedes the method, either as a selector expression or as markup created on the fly, and it is inserted after the target container.

Consider the following HTML:

```
<div class="demo-container">
  <div class="demo-box">Demonstration Box
  </div>
</div>
```

The two `<div>`s, with a little CSS, are rendered on the right side of the page as follows:

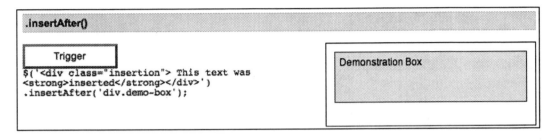

Using `.insertAfter()`, we can insert an HTML structure after `<div class="demo-box">` like so:

```
$('<div class="insertion">This text was <strong>inserted</strong>
                          </div>').insertAfter('div.demo-box');
```

The new `<div>` and `<strong>` elements, as well as the text nodes, are created on the fly and added to the DOM. The result is a new `<div>` positioned outside of, just after, `<div class="demo-box">`:

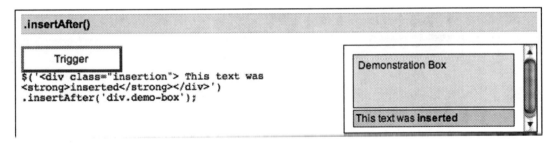

An element (or array of elements) that already exists on the page could be moved to the DOM position just after `<div class="demo-box">` as well. The following code, for example, moves the document's first paragraph by using a jQuery object:

```
$('p:eq(0)').insertAfter('div.demo-box');
```

DOM Insertion, Around

.wrap()

> Wraps a structure of elements around each element in the set of matched elements.
>
>   .wrap(html)
>
>   .wrap(element)

Parameters (first version)

- html: A string of HTML tags to wrap around the set of matched elements

Parameters (second version)

- element: An existing element to wrap around the set of matched elements

Return Value

The jQuery object, for chaining purposes.

Description

Note: The HTML must include only well-formed, valid element structures. If any text is included, or if any tags are left unclosed, the `.wrap()` will fail.

Consider the following HTML:

```
<div class="demo-container">
  <div class="demo-box">Demonstration Box
  </div>
</div>
```

The two `<div>`s, with a little CSS, are rendered on the right side of the page as follows:

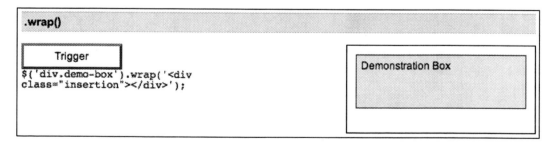

Using `.wrap()`, we can insert an HTML structure around `<div class="demo-box">` like so:

```
$('div.demo-box').wrap('<div class="insertion"> </div>');
```

The new `<div>` element is created on the fly and added to the DOM. The result is a new `<div>` wrapped around `<div class="demo-box">`:

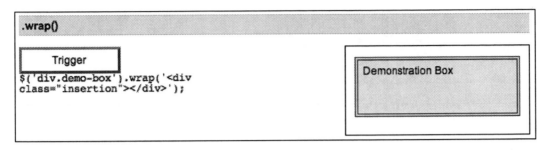

Using a DOM node as our parameter instead, we could wrap the new `<div>` around an element with `id="demo-box1"` like so:

```
$(document.getElementById('demo-box1')).wrap('
                              <div class="insertion"> </div>');
```

DOM Copying

.clone()

Creates a copy of the set of matched elements.

```
.clone([deep])
```

Parameters
- deep (optional): A Boolean. Default is `true`. If set to `false`, the `.clone` method copies only the matched elements themselves, excluding any child/descendant elements and text.

Return Value
A new jQuery object, referencing the created elements.

Description

The `.clone` method, when used in conjunction with one of the insertion methods, is a convenient way to duplicate elements on a page. Consider the following HTML:

```html
<div class="demo-container">
  <div class="demo-box">Demonstration Box
  </div>
</div>
```

The two `<div>`s, with a little CSS, are rendered on the right side of the page as follows:

```
.clone()

  Trigger
$('div.demo-box:last').clone()
.insertAfter('div.demo-box:last');

                                    Demonstration Box
```

To copy `<div class="demo-box">` and paste that copy after the original, we could write the following:

```
$('div.demo-box:last').clone().insertAfter('div.demo-box:last');
```

Now we have **Demonstration Box twice**:

```
.clone()

  Trigger
$('div.demo-box:last').clone()
.insertAfter('div.demo-box:last');

                                    Demonstration Box

                                    Demonstration Box
```

Notice that we use the `:last` selector here so that we are sure to only copy (`.clone()`) and paste (`.insertAfter()`) a single copy. We need to be aware of the potential to inadvertently clone or insert more than we intend, and take the necessary precautions to prevent that from occurring.

> With the `.clone` method, we can modify the cloned elements or their contents before inserting them into the document.

The optional `deep` parameter accepts a Boolean—`true` or `false`. Since in most cases we want to clone child nodes as well, and since the default is `true`, the parameter is rarely used. However, imagine that we wanted to copy the **Demonstration Box** without its text and then append a paragraph to every `<div class="demo-box">`. We could make this happen with the following code:

```
$('div.demo-box:last').clone(false).insertAfter('div.demo-box:last');
$('div.demo-box').append('<p>New Message</p>');
```

Now the two boxes look like this:

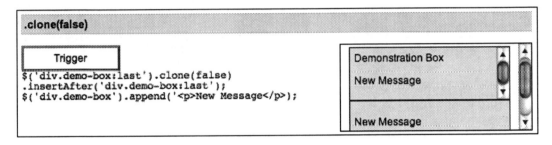

The first box now has both the original **Demonstration Box** text and the additional **New Message** text while the new, cloned box has only the additional text.

DOM Removal

.empty()

> Removes all child nodes of the set of matched elements from the DOM.
>
> ```
> .empty()
> ```

Parameters

None.

Return Value

The jQuery object, for chaining purposes.

Description

This method removes not only child (and other descendant) elements, but also any text within the set of matched elements. This is because, according to the DOM, any string of text within an element is considered a child node of that element. Consider the following HTML:

```
<div class="demo-container">
  <div class="demo-box">Demonstration Box
  </div>
</div>
```

The two <div>s, with a little CSS, are rendered on the right side of the page as follows:

If we apply `$('div.demo-box').empty();` to it, the **Demonstration Box** text string is removed:

If we had any number of nested elements inside <div class="demo-box">, they would be removed, too.

.remove()

Removes the set of matched elements from the DOM.

```
.remove([selector])
```

Parameters

- selector (optional): A selector that filters the set of matched elements to be removed

Return Value

The jQuery object, for chaining purposes.

Description

Similar to .empty, the .remove method takes elements out of the DOM. We use .remove() when we want to remove the element itself, as well as everything inside it. Consider the following HTML:

```
<div class="demo-container">
  <div class="demo-box">Demonstration Box
  </div>
</div>
```

The two <div>s, with a little CSS, are rendered on the right side of the page as follows:

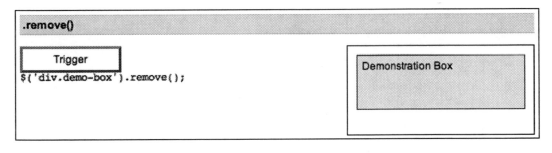

If we apply $('div.demo-box').remove() to it, the entire <div class="demo-box> along with everything in it is removed:

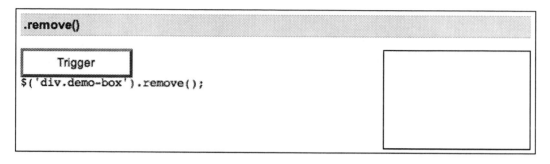

We can also include a selector as an optional parameter. For example, we could rewrite the previous DOM removal code as follows: $('div').remove('.demo-box'). Or, if we had multiple elements with the same class name and wanted to remove only the first one the one with id="temporary-demo-box", we could write the following:

```
$('div.demo-box').remove('#temporary-demo-box ').
```

5
Event Methods

Woman, I am bound to you
What will I do?
                        — Devo,
         "The Rope Song"

In this chapter, we'll closely examine each of the available event methods in turn. These methods are used to register behaviors to take effect when the user interacts with the browser, and to further manipulate those registered behaviors.

Event Handler Attachment

The following methods are the building blocks of jQuery's event handling module.

.bind()

Attaches a handler to an event for the elements

```
.bind(eventType[, eventData], handler)
```

Parameters

- eventType: A string containing a JavaScript event type, such as `click` or `submit`

- eventData (optional): A map of data that will be passed to the event handler

- handler: A function to execute each time the event is triggered

Return Value

The jQuery object, for chaining purposes.

Description

The `.bind()` method is the primary means of attaching behavior to a document. All JavaScript event types are allowed for *eventType*; the following are cross-platform and recommended:

- `blur`
- `change`
- `click`
- `dblclick`
- `error`
- `focus`
- `keydown`
- `keypress`
- `keyup`
- `load`
- `mousedown`
- `mousemove`
- `mouseout`
- `mouseover`
- `mouseup`
- `resize`
- `scroll`
- `select`
- `submit`
- `unload`

The jQuery library provides shortcut methods for binding each of these event types, such as `.click()` for `.bind('click')`. Descriptions of each event type can be found in the description of its shortcut method.

When an event reaches an element, all handlers bound to that event type for the element are fired. If there are multiple handlers registered, they will always execute in the order in which they were bound. After all handlers have executed, the event continues along the normal event propagation path. For a full discussion of event propagation, see *Learning jQuery* or the W3C specification at `http://www.w3.org/TR/DOM-Level-2-Event/`. A basic usage of `.bind()` is:

```
$('#foo').bind('click', function() {
  alert('User clicked on "foo."');
});
```

This code will cause the element with an ID of `foo` to respond to the `click` event; when a user clicks inside this element thereafter, the alert will be shown.

Event Handlers

The `handler` parameter takes a callback function, as shown; within the handler, the keyword `this` is set to the DOM element to which the handler is bound. To make use of the element in jQuery, it can be passed to the normal `$()` function. For example:

```
$('#foo').bind('click', function() {
  alert($(this).text());
});
```

After this code is executed, when the user clicks inside the element with an ID of `foo`, its text contents will be shown as an alert.

The Event Object

The callback function takes a single parameter; when the handler is called the JavaScript event object will be passed through it.

The event object is often unneccessary and the parameter is omitted, as sufficient context is usually available when the handler is bound to know exactly what needs to be done when the handler is triggered. However, at times it becomes necessary to gather more information about the user's environment at the time the event was initiated. JavaScript provides information such as `.shiftKey` (whether the *shift* key was held down at the time), `.offsetX` (the *x* coordinate of the mouse cursor within the element), and `.type` (the kind of event this is).

Some of the event object's attributes and methods are not available on every platform. If the event is handled by a jQuery event handler, however, the library standardizes certain attributes so that they can be safely used on any browser. In particular:

- `.target`: This attribute represents the DOM element that initiated the event. It is often useful to compare `event.target` to `this` in order to determine if the event is being handled due to event bubbling.

- .pageX: This attribute contains the *x* coordinate of the mouse cursor relative to the left edge of the page.

- .pageY: This attribute contains the *y* coordinate of the mouse cursor relative to the top edge of the page.

- .preventDefault(): If this method is called, the default action of the event will not be triggered. For example, clicked anchors will not take the browser to a new URL.

- .stopPropagation(): This method prevents the event from bubbling up the DOM tree looking for more event handlers to trigger.

Returning false from a handler is equivalent to calling both .preventDefault() and .stopPropagation() on the event object.

Using the event object in a handler looks like this:

```
$(document).ready(function() {
  $('#foo').bind('click', function(event) {
    alert('The mouse cursor is at (' + event.pageX + ', ' +
                                        event.pageY + ')');
  });
});
```

Note the parameter added to the anonymous function. This code will cause a click on the element with ID foo to report the page coordinates of the mouse cursor at the time of the click.

Passing Event Data

The optional *eventData* parameter is not commonly used. When provided, this argument allows us to pass additional information to the handler. One handy use of this parameter is to work around the issues caused by closures. For example, suppose we have two event handlers where both refer to the same external variable:

```
var message = 'Spoon!';
$('#foo').bind('click', function() {
  alert(message);
});
message = 'Not in the face!';
$('#bar').bind('click', function() {
  alert(message);
});
```

Because the handlers are closures that both have message in their environment, both will display the message Not in the face! when triggered. The variable's value has changed. To sidestep this, we can pass the message in eventData:

```
var message = 'Spoon!';
$('#foo').bind('click', {msg: message}, function(event) {
  alert(event.data.msg);
});
message = 'Not in the face!';
$('#bar').bind('click', {msg: message}, function(event) {
  alert(event.data.msg);
});
```

This time the variable is not referred to directly within the handlers; instead, the value is passed in through eventData, which fixes the value at the time the event is bound. The first handler will now display Spoon! while the second will alert Not in the face!

If *eventData* is present, it is the second argument to the .bind() method; if no additional data needs to be sent to the handler, then the callback is passed as the second and final argument.

 See the .trigger() method reference for a way to pass data to a handler at the time the event happens rather than when the handler is bound.

.unbind()

Removes a previously attached event handler from the elements.

```
.unbind([eventType[, handler]])
```

```
.unbind(event)
```

Parameters (First Version)

- eventType: A string containing a JavaScript event type, such as click or submit
- handler: The function that is no longer to be executed

Parameters (Second Version)

- event: A JavaScript event object as passed to an event handler

Return Value

The jQuery object, for chaining purposes.

Description

Any handler that has been attached with `.bind()` can be removed with `.unbind()`. In the simplest case, with no arguments, `.unbind()` removes all handlers attached to the elements:

```
$('#foo').unbind();
```

This version removes the handlers regardless of type. To be more precise, we can pass an event type:

```
$('#foo').unbind('click');
```

By specifying the "click" event type, only handlers for that event type will be unbound. This approach can still have negative ramifications if other scripts might be attaching behaviors to the same element, however. Robust and extensible applications typically demand the two-argument version for this reason:

```
var handler = function() {

    alert('The quick brown fox jumps over the lazy dog.');

};

$('#foo').bind('click', handler);

$('#foo').unbind('click', handler);
```

By naming the handler, we can be assured that no other functions are caught in the crossfire. Note that the following will *not* work:

```
$('#foo').bind('click', function() {
    alert('The quick brown fox jumps over the lazy dog.');
});

$('#foo').unbind('click', function() {
    alert('The quick brown fox jumps over the lazy dog.');
});
```

Even though the two functions are identical in content, they are created separately and so JavaScript is free to keep them as distinct function objects. To unbind a particular handler, we need a reference to that function and not to a different one that happens to do the same thing.

Using the Event Object

The second form of this method is used when we wish to unbind a handler from within itself. For example, suppose we wish to trigger an event handler only three times:

```
var timesClicked = 0;
$('#foo').bind('click', function(event) {
  alert('The quick brown fox jumps over the lazy dog.');
  timesClicked++;
  if (timesClicked >= 3) {
    $(this).unbind(event);
  }
});
```

The handler in this case must take a parameter, so that we can capture the event object and use it to unbind the handler after the third click. The event object contains the context necessary for `.unbind()` to know which handler to remove.

This example is also an illustration of a closure. Since the handler refers to the `timesClicked` variable, which is defined outside the function, incrementing the variable has an effect even between invocations of the handler.

.one()

Attaches a handler to an event for the elements. The handler is executed at most once.

```
.one(eventType[, eventData], handler)
```

Parameters

- eventType: A string containing a JavaScript event type, such as `click` or `submit`
- eventData (optional): A map of data that will be passed to the event handler
- handler: A function to execute at the time the event is triggered

Return Value

The jQuery object, for chaining purposes.

Description

This method is identical to `.bind()`, except that the handler is unbound after its first invocation. For example:

```
$('#foo').one('click', function() {
  alert('This will be displayed only once.');
});
```

After the code is executed, a click on the element with ID `foo` will display the alert. Subsequent clicks will do nothing.

This code is equivalent to:

```
$('#foo').bind('click', function(event) {
  alert('This will be displayed only once.');
  $(this).unbind(event);
});
```

In other words, explicitly calling `.unbind()` from within a regularly bound handler has exactly the same effect.

.trigger()

Executes all handlers attached to an element for an event.

`.trigger(eventType [, extraParameters])`

Parameters

- eventType: A string containing a JavaScript event type, such as `click` or `submit`

- extraParameters: An array of additional parameters to pass along to the event handler

Return Value

The jQuery object, for chaining purposes.

Description

Any event handlers attached with `.bind()` or one of its shortcut methods are triggered when the corresponding event occurs. They can be fired manually, however, with the `.trigger()` method. A call to `.trigger()` executes the handlers in the same order they would be if the event were triggered naturally by the user:

```
$('#foo').bind('click', function() {
  alert($(this).text());
});
$('#foo').trigger('click');
```

While .trigger() simulates an event activation, complete with a synthesized event object, it does not perfectly replicate a naturally-occurring event. No event bubbling occurs, so the .trigger() call must be made on the element that actually has the event handlers attached. Default behaviors are also not reliably invoked, so must be called manually with methods such as .submit() on the DOM elements themselves.

When we define a custom event type using the .bind() method, the second argument to .trigger() can become useful. For example, suppose we have bound a handler for the custom event to our element instead of the built-in click event as we did previously:

```
$('#foo').bind('custom', function(event, param1, param2) {
  alert(param1 + "\n" + param2);
});
$('#foo').trigger('custom', ['Custom', 'Event']);
```

The event object is always passed as the first parameter to an event handler, but if additional parameters are specified during a .trigger() call as they are here, these parameters will be passed along to the handler as well.

Note the difference between the extra parameters we're passing here and the eventData parameter to the .bind() method. Both are mechanisms for passing information to an event handler, but the extraParameters argument to .trigger() allows information to be determined at the time the event is triggered while the eventData argument to .bind() requires the information to be already computed at the time the handler is bound.

Document Loading

These events deal with the loading of a page into the browser.

$()

Specifies a function to execute when the DOM is fully loaded
```
$(document).ready(handler)
$().ready(handler)
$(handler)
```

Parameters
- handler: A function to execute after the DOM is ready

Return Value

The jQuery object, for chaining purposes.

Description

While JavaScript provides the `load` event for executing code when a page is rendered, this event does not get triggered until all assets such as images have been completely received. In most cases, the script can be run as soon as the DOM hierarchy has been fully constructed. The handler passed to `.ready()` is guaranteed to be executed after the DOM is ready, so this is usually the best place to attach all other event handlers and run other jQuery code.

In cases where code relies on loaded assets (for example, if the dimensions of an image are required), the code should be placed in a handler for the `load` event instead.

The `.ready()` method is generally incompatible with the `<body onload="">` attribute. If `load` must be used, either do not use `.ready()` or use jQuery's `.load()` method to attach `load` event handlers to the window or to more specific items, like images.

All three syntaxes provided are equivalent. The `.ready()` method can only be called on a jQuery object matching the current document, so the selector can be omitted.

The `.ready()` method is typically used with an anonymous function:

```
$(document).ready(function() {
  alert('Ready event was triggered.');
});
```

With this code in place, an alert will be displayed when the page is loaded.

When using another JavaScript library, we may wish to call `$.noConflict()` to avoid namespace difficulties. When this function is called, the `$` shortcut is no longer available, forcing us to write `jQuery` each time we would normally write `$`. However, the handler passed to the `.ready()` method can take an argument, which is passed the global jQuery object. This means we can rename the object within the context of our `.ready()` handler without affecting other code:

```
jQuery(document).ready(function($) {
  // Code using $ as usual goes here.
});
```

If `.ready()` is called after the DOM has been initialized, the new handler passed in will be executed immediately.

.load()

Binds an event handler to the load JavaScript event.

    .load(handler)

Parameters

- handler: A function to execute when the event is triggered

Return Value

The jQuery object, for chaining purposes.

Description

This handler is a shortcut for `.bind('load', handler)`.

The `load` event is sent to an element when it and all sub-elements have been completely loaded. This event can be sent to any element associated with a URL—images, scripts, frames, and the body of the document itself.

For example, consider the HTML:

```
<img class="target" src="hat.gif" width="80" height="54" alt="Hat" />
```

The event handler can be bound to the image:

```
$('.target').load(function() {
  $(this).log('Load event was triggered.');
});
```

Now as soon as the image has been loaded, the message is displayed.

In general, it is not necessary to wait for all images to be fully loaded. If code can be executed earlier, it is usually best to place it in a handler sent to the `.ready()` method.

 The AJAX module also has a method named `.load()`. Which one is fired depends on the set of arguments passed.

.unload()

Binds an event handler to the unload JavaScript event.

```
.unload(handler)
```

Parameters

- handler: A function to execute when the event is triggered.

Return Value

The jQuery object, for chaining purposes.

Description

This handler is a shortcut for `.bind('unload', handler)`.

The `unload` event is sent to the `window` element when the user has navigated away from the page. This could mean one of many things. The user could have clicked on a link to leave the page, or typed in a new URL in the address bar. The forward and back buttons will trigger the event. Closing the browser window will cause the event to be triggered. Even a page reload will first create an `unload` event.

Any `unload` event handler should be bound to the `window` object:

```
$(window).unload(function() {
  alert('Unload event was triggered.');
});
```

After this code executes, the alert will be displayed whenever the browser leaves the current page.

It is not possible to cancel the `unload` event with `.preventDefault()`. This event is available so that scripts can perform cleanup when the user leaves the page.

.error()

Binds an event handler to the error JavaScript event.

```
.error(handler)
```

Parameters

- handler: A function to execute when the event is triggered

Return Value

The jQuery object, for chaining purposes.

Description

This handler is a shortcut for `.bind('error', handler)`.

The `error` event is sent to the same elements that can receive the `load` event. It is called if the element was not loaded correctly.

For example, consider the HTML:

```
<img class="target" src="missing.gif" width="80" height="54"
                                        alt="Missing Image" />
```

The event handler can be bound to the image:

```
$('.target').error(function() {
  $(this).log('Error event was triggered.');
});
```

If the image cannot be loaded (for example, because it is not present at the supplied URL), the message is displayed.

This event may not be correctly fired when the page is served locally. Since `error` relies on normal HTTP status codes, it will generally not be triggered if the URL uses the `file:` protocol.

Mouse Events

These events are triggered by mouse movement and button presses.

.mousedown()

Binds an event handler to the mousedown JavaScript event, or triggers that event on an element.

.mousedown(handler)

.mousedown()

Parameters (First Version)

- handler: A function to execute each time the event is triggered

Return Value

The jQuery object, for chaining purposes.

Description

This handler is a shortcut for `.bind('mousedown', handler)` in the first variation, and `.trigger('mousedown')` in the second.

The `mousedown` event is sent to an element when the mouse pointer is over the element, and the mouse button is pressed. Any HTML element can receive this event.

For example, consider the HTML:

```
<div class="target button">Click Here</div>
<div class="trigger button">Trigger</div>
```

The event handler can be bound to the target button:

```
$('.target').mousedown(function() {
  $(this).log('Mousedown event was triggered.');
});
```

Now if we click on the target button, the message is displayed. We can also trigger the event when the second button is clicked:

```
$('.trigger').click(function() {
  $('.target').mousedown();
});
```

After this code executes, clicks on the trigger button will also display the message.

The `mousedown` event is sent when any mouse button is clicked. To act only on specific buttons, we can use the event object's `which` property in Mozilla browsers (1 for left button, 2 for middle button, 3 for right button), or the `button` property in Internet Explorer (1 for left button, 4 for middle button, 2 for right button). This is primarily useful for ensuring that the primary button was used to begin a drag operation; if ignored, strange results can occur when the user attempts to use a context menu. While the middle and right buttons can be detected with these properties, this is not reliable. In Opera and Safari, for example, right mouse button clicks are not detectable by default.

If the user clicks on an element, then drags the mouse pointer away from it or releases the button, this is still counted as a mousedown event. This sequence of actions is treated as a *canceling* of the button press in most user interfaces, so it is usually better to use the click event unless we know that the mousedown event is preferable for a particular situation.

.mouseup()

> Binds an event handler to the mouseup JavaScript event, or triggers that event on an element.
>
> .mouseup(handler)
>
> .mouseup()

Parameters (First Version)

- handler: A function to execute each time the event is triggered

Return Value

The jQuery object, for chaining purposes.

Description

This handler is a shortcut for .bind('mouseup', handler) in the first variation, and .trigger('mouseup') in the second.

The mouseup event is sent to an element when the mouse pointer is over the element, and the mouse button is released. Any HTML element can receive this event.

For example, consider the HTML:

```
<div class="target button">Click Here</div>
<div class="trigger button">Trigger</div>
```

The event handler can be bound to the target button:

```
$('.target').mouseup(function() {
  $(this).log('Mouseup event was triggered.');
});
```

Now if we click on the target button, the message is displayed. We can also trigger the event when the second button is clicked:

```
$('.trigger').click(function() {
  $('.target').mouseup();
});
```

After this code executes, clicking the **Trigger** button will also display the message.

If the user clicks outside an element, drags onto it, and releases the button, this is still counted as a mouseup event. This sequence of actions is not treated as a button press in most user interfaces, so it is usually better to use the click event unless we know that the mouseup event is preferable for a particular situation.

.click()

Binds an event handler to the click JavaScript event, or triggers that event on an element.

```
.click(handler)
.click()
```

Parameters (First Version)
- handler: A function to execute each time the event is triggered

Return Value
The jQuery object, for chaining purposes.

Description
This handler is a shortcut for .bind('click', handler) in the first variation, and .trigger('click') in the second.

The click event is sent to an element when the mouse pointer is over the element, and the mouse button is pressed and released. Any HTML element can receive this event.

For example, consider the HTML:

```
<div class="target button">Click Here</div>
<div class="trigger button">Trigger</div>
```

The event handler can be bound to the target button:

```
$('.target').click(function() {
  $(this).log('Click event was triggered.');
});
```

Now if we click on the target button, the message is displayed. We can also trigger the event when the second button is clicked:

```
$('.trigger').click(function() {
  $('.target').click();
});
```

After this code executes, clicking the trigger button will also display the message.

The `click` event is only triggered after this exact series of events:

- The mouse button is depressed while the pointer is inside the element.
- The mouse button is released while the pointer is inside the element.

This is usually the desired sequence before taking an action. If this is not required, the `mousedown` or `mouseup` event may be more suitable.

.dblclick()

> Binds an event handler to the `dblclick` JavaScript event, or triggers that event on an element.
>
>   .dblclick(handler)
>
>   .dblclick()

Parameters (First Version)

- handler: A function to execute each time the event is triggered

Return Value

The jQuery object, for chaining purposes.

Description

This handler is a shortcut for `.bind('dblclick', handler)` in the first variation, and `.trigger('dblclick')` in the second.

The `dblclick` event is sent to an element when the element is double-clicked. Any HTML element can receive this event.

For example, consider the HTML:

```
<div class="target button">Click Here</div>
<div class="trigger button">Trigger</div>
```

The event handler can be bound to the target button:

```
$('.target').dblclick(function() {
  $(this).log('Dblclick event was triggered.');
});
```

Now if we double-click on the target button, the message is displayed. We can also trigger the event when the second button is clicked:

```
$('.trigger').click(function() {
  $('.target').dblclick();
});
```

After this code executes, clicking the **Trigger** button will also display the message.

The `dblclick` event is only triggered after this exact series of events:

- The mouse button is depressed while the pointer is inside the element.
- The mouse button is released while the pointer is inside the element.
- The mouse button is depressed again while the pointer is inside the element, within a time window that is system-dependent.
- The mouse button is released while the pointer is inside the element.

It is inadvisable to bind handlers to both the `click` and `dblclick` events for the same element. The sequence of events triggered varies from browser to browser, with some receiving two `click` events and others only one. If an interface that reacts differently to single and double clicks cannot be avoided, then the `dblclick` event should be simulated within the `click` handler. We can achieve this by saving a timestamp in the handler, and then comparing the current time to the saved timestamp on subsequent clicks. If the difference is small enough, we can treat the click as a double-click.

.toggle()

> Binds two event handlers to the matched elements, to be executed on alternate clicks.
>
> ```
> .toggle(handlerEven, handlerOdd)
> ```

Parameters

- handlerEven: A function to execute every even time the element is clicked.
- handlerOdd: A function to execute every odd time the element is clicked.

Return Value

The jQuery object, for chaining purposes.

Description

The `.toggle()` method binds a handler for the `click` event, so the rules outlined for the triggering of `click` apply here as well.

For example, consider the HTML:

```
<div class="target button">Click Here</div>
```

The event handlers can be bound to this button:

```
$('.target').toggle(function() {
  $(this).log('Toggle event was triggered (handler 1).');
}, function() {
  $(this).log('Toggle event was triggered (handler 2).');
});
```

The first time the button is clicked, the first handler will be executed. The second time, the second handler will execute. Subsequent clicks will cycle between the two handlers.

The `.toggle()` method is provided for convenience. It is relatively straightforward to implement the same behavior by hand, and this can be necessary if the assumptions built into `.toggle()` prove limiting. For example, `.toggle()` is not guaranteed to work correctly if applied twice to the same element. Since `.toggle()` internally uses a `click` handler to do its work, we must unbind `click` to remove a behavior attached with `.toggle()`, so other `click` handlers can be caught in the crossfire. The implementation also calls `.preventDefault()` on the event, so links will not be followed and buttons will not be clicked if `.toggle()` has been called on the element.

.mouseover()

> Binds an event handler to the mouseover JavaScript event, or triggers that event on an element.
>
> ```
> .mouseover(handler)
> ```
> ```
> .mouseover()
> ```

Parameters (First Version)

- handler: A function to execute each time the event is triggered

Return Value

The jQuery object, for chaining purposes.

Description

This handler is a shortcut for `.bind('mouseover', handler)` in the first variation, and `.trigger('mouseover')` in the second.

The `mouseover` event is sent to an element when the mouse pointer enters the element. Any HTML element can receive this event.

For example, consider the HTML:

```
<div class="target button">Move Here</div>
<div class="trigger button">Trigger</div>
```

The event handler can be bound to the target button:

```
$('.target').mouseover(function() {
  $(this).log('Mouseover event was triggered.');
});
```

Now when the mouse pointer moves over the target button, the message is displayed. We can also trigger the event when the second button is clicked:

```
$('.trigger').click(function() {
  $('.target').mouseover();
});
```

After this code executes, clicking the **Trigger** button will also display the message.

This event type can cause many headaches due to event bubbling. When the mouse pointer moves over a nested element, a `mouseover` event will be sent to that, then trickle up the hierarchy. This can trigger our bound `mouseover` handler at inopportune times. By using the `.hover()` method instead, we can avoid this problem.

.mouseout()

Bind an event handler to the **mouseout** JavaScript event, or trigger that event on an element.

```
.mouseout(handler)
```

```
.mouseout()
```

Parameters (First Version)

- handler: A function to execute each time the event is triggered

Return Value

The jQuery object, for chaining purposes.

Description

This handler is a shortcut for `.bind('mouseout', handler)` in the first variation, and `.trigger('mouseout')` in the second.

The `mouseout` event is sent to an element when the mouse pointer leaves the element. Any HTML element can receive this event.

For example, consider the HTML:

```
<div class="target button">Move Here</div>
<div class="trigger button">Trigger</div>
```

The event handler can be bound to the target button:

```
$('.target').mouseout(function() {
  $(this).log('Mouseout event was triggered.');
});
```

Now when the mouse pointer moves out of the target button, the message is displayed. We can also trigger the event when the second button is clicked:

```
$('.trigger').click(function() {
  $('.target').mouseout();
});
```

After this code executes, clicking the **Trigger** button will also display the message.

This event type can cause many headaches due to event bubbling. When the mouse pointer moves out of a nested element, a `mouseout` event will be sent to that, then trickle up the hierarchy. This can trigger our bound `mouseout` handler at inopportune times. By using the `.hover()` method instead, we can avoid this problem.

.hover()

Binds two event handlers to the matched elements, to be executed when the mouse pointer enters and leaves the elements.

```
.hover(handlerIn, handlerOut)
```

Parameters

- handlerIn: A function to execute when the mouse pointer enters the element
- handlerOut: A function to execute when the mouse pointer leaves the element

Return Value

The jQuery object, for chaining purposes.

Description

The `.hover()` method binds handlers for both `mouseover` and `mouseout` events. We can use it to simply apply behavior to an element during the time the mouse is within the element. Consider the HTML:

```
<div class="target button">Move Here</div>
```

Now we can bind handlers to both entering the element and leaving it with a single method call:

```
$('.target').hover(function() {
  $(this).log('Hover event was triggered (entering).');
}, function() {
  $(this).log('Hover event was triggered (leaving).');
});
```

Now the first message will be displayed when the mouse pointer enters the element, and the second will be displayed when the mouse pointer leaves.

With the `mouseover` and `mouseout` events, it is common to receive false positives due to event bubbling. When the mouse pointer crosses over a nested element, the events are generated and will bubble up to the parent element. The `.hover()` method incorporates code to check for this situation and do nothing, so we can safely ignore this problem when using the `.hover()` shortcut.

.mousemove()

Binds an event handler to the mousemove JavaScript event, or triggers that event on an element.

```
.mousemove(handler)
```
```
.mousemove()
```

Parameters (First Version)
- handler: A function to execute each time the event is triggered

Return Value

The jQuery object, for chaining purposes.

Description

This handler is a shortcut for `.bind('mousemove', handler)` in the first variation, and `.trigger('mousemove')` in the second.

The `mousemove` event is sent to an element when the mouse pointer moves inside the element. Any HTML element can receive this event.

For example, consider the HTML:

```
<div class="target button">Move Here</div>
<div class="trigger button">Trigger</div>
```

The event handler can be bound to the target button:

```
$('.target').mousemove(function() {
  $(this).log('Mousemove event was triggered.');
});
```

Now when the mouse pointer moves within the target button, the message is displayed. We can also trigger the event when the second button is clicked:

```
$('.trigger').click(function() {
  $('.target').mousemove();
});
```

After this code executes, clicking the **Trigger** button will also display the message.

When tracking the mouse movement, we usually clearly need to know the actual position of the mouse pointer. The event object that is passed to the handler contains some information about the mouse coordinates. Properties such as `.clientX`, `.offsetX`, and `.pageX` are available, but support for them differs between browsers. Fortunately, jQuery normalizes the `.pageX` and `.pageY` attributes so that they can be used in all browsers. These attributes provide the x and y coordinates of the mouse pointer relative to the top-left corner of the page.

We need to remember that the `mousemove` event is triggered whenever the mouse pointer moves, even for a pixel. This means that hundreds of events can be generated over a very small amount of time. If the handler has to do any significant processing, or if multiple handlers for the event exist, this can be a serious performance drain on the browser. It is important, therefore, to optimize `mousemove` handlers as much as possible, and to unbind them as soon as they are no longer needed.

A common pattern is to bind the mousemove handler from within a mousedown hander, and to unbind it from a corresponding mouseup handler. If implementing this sequence of events, remember that the mouseup event might be sent to a different HTML element than the mousemove event was. To account for this, the mouseup handler should typically be bound to an element high up in the DOM tree, such as <body>.

Form Events

These events refer to <form> elements and their contents.

.focus()

Binds an event handler to the focus JavaScript event, or triggers that event on an element.

> .focus(handler)
>
> .focus()

Parameters (First Version)

- handler: A function to execute each time the event is triggered

Return Value

The jQuery object, for chaining purposes.

Description

This handler is a shortcut for .bind('focus', handler) in the first variation, and .trigger('focus') in the second.

The focus event is sent to an element when it gains focus. Originally, this event was only applicable to form elements, such as <input>. In recent browsers, the domain of the event has been extended to include all element types. An element can gain focus via keyboard commands, such as the *Tab* key, or by mouse clicks on the element.

Elements with focus are usually highlighted in some way by the browser, for example with a dotted line surrounding the element. The focus is used to determine which element is the first to receive keyboard-related events.

For example, consider the HTML:

```
<form>
  <input class="target" type="text" value="Field 1" />
```

```
  <input type="text" value="Field 2" />
</form>
<div class="trigger button">Trigger</div>
```

The event handler can be bound to the first input field:

```
$('.target').focus(function() {
  $(this).log('Focus event was triggered.');
});
```

Now if we click on the first field, or *Tab* to it from another field, the message is displayed. We can trigger the event when the button is clicked:

```
$('.trigger').click(function() {
  $('.target').focus();
});
```

After this code executes, clicking the **Trigger** button will also display the message.

> Triggering the focus on hidden elements causes an error in Internet Explorer. Take care to only call .focus() without parameters on elements that are visible.

.blur()

> Binds an event handler to the blur JavaScript event, or triggers that event on an element.
>
>   .blur(handler)
>
>   .blur()

Parameters (First Version)

- handler: A function to execute each time the event is triggered

Return Value

The jQuery object, for chaining purposes.

Description

This handler is a shortcut for .bind('blur', handler) in the first variation, and .trigger('blur') in the second.

The `blur` event is sent to an element when it loses focus. Originally, this event was only applicable to form elements, such as `<input>`. In recent browsers, the domain of the event has been extended to include all element types. An element can lose focus via keyboard commands, such as the *Tab* key, or by mouse clicks elsewhere on the page.

For example, consider the HTML:

```
<form>
  <input class="target" type="text" value="Field 1" />
  <input type="text" value="Field 2" />
</form>
<div class="trigger button">Trigger</div>
```

The event handler can be bound to the first input field:

```
$('.target').blur(function() {
  $(this).log('Blur event was triggered.');
});
```

Now if we click on the first field, then click or tab away, the message is displayed. We can trigger the event when the button is clicked:

```
$('.trigger').click(function() {
  $('.target').blur();
});
```

After this code executes, clicking the **Trigger** button will also display the message.

.change()

> Binds an event handler to the change JavaScript event, or triggers that event on an element.
>
> `.change(handler)`
>
> `.change()`

Parameters (First Version)

- handler: A function to execute each time the event is triggered

Return Value

The jQuery object, for chaining purposes.

Description

This handler is a shortcut for `.bind('change', handler)` in the first variation, and `.trigger('change')` in the second.

The change event is sent to an element when its value changes. This event is limited to `<input type="text">` fields, `<textarea>` boxes, and `<select>` elements. For select boxes, the event is fired immediately when the user makes a selection with the mouse, but for the other element types the event is deferred until the element loses focus.

For example, consider the HTML:

```
<form>
  <input class="target" type="text" value="Field 1" />
  <select class="target">
    <option value="option1" selected="selected">Option 1</option>
    <option value="option2">Option 2</option>
  </select>
</form>
<div class="trigger button">Trigger</div>
```

The event handler can be bound to the text input and the select box:

```
$('.target').change(function() {
  $(this).log('Change event was triggered.');
});
```

Now when the second option is selected from the dropdown, the message is displayed. It is also displayed if we change the text in the field and then click away. If the field loses focus without the contents having changed, though, the event is not triggered. We can trigger the event manually when the button is clicked:

```
$('.trigger').click(function() {
  $('.target').change();
});
```

After this code executes, clicks on the trigger button will also display the message. The message will be displayed twice, because the handler has been bound to the change event on both of the form elements.

.select()

Binds an event handler to the select JavaScript event, or triggers that event on an element.

        .select(handler)

        .select()

Parameters (First Version)

- handler: A function to execute each time the event is triggered

Return Value

The jQuery object, for chaining purposes.

Description

This handler is a shortcut for `.bind('select', handler)` in the first variation, and `.trigger('select')` in the second.

The `select` event is sent to an element when the user makes a text selection inside it. This event is limited to `<input type="text">` fields and `<textarea>` boxes.

For example, consider the HTML:

```
<form>
  <input class="target" type="text" value="The quick brown fox jumps
                                       over the lazy dog." />
</form>
<div class="trigger button">Trigger</div>
```

The event handler can be bound to the text input:

```
$('.target').select(function() {
  $(this).log('Select event was triggered.');
});
```

Now when any portion of the text is selected, the message is displayed. Merely setting the location of the insertion point will not trigger the event. We can trigger the event manually when the button is clicked:

```
$('.trigger').click(function() {
  $('.target').select();
});
```

After this code executes, clicking the **Trigger** button will also display the message. In addition, the default `select` action on the field will be fired, so the entire text field will be selected.

.submit()

> Binds an event handler to the submit JavaScript event, or triggers that event on an element.
>
> ```
> .submit(handler)
> ```
> ```
> .submit()
> ```

Parameters (First Version)

- handler: A function to execute each time the event is triggered

Return Value

The jQuery object, for chaining purposes.

Description

This handler is a shortcut for `.bind('submit', handler)` in the first variation, and `.trigger('submit')` in the second.

The `submit` event is sent to an element when the user is attempting to submit a form. It can only be attached to `<form>` elements. Forms can be submitted either by clicking an explicit `<input type="submit">` button, or by pressing *Enter* when a form element has focus.

 Depending on the browser, the *Enter* key may only cause a form submission if the form has exactly one text field, or only when there is a submit button present. The interface should not rely on a particular behavior for this key unless the issue is forced by observing the `keypress` event for presses of the *Enter* key.

For example, consider the HTML:

```
<form class="target" action="foo.html">
  <input type="text" />
  <input type="submit" value="Go" />
</form>
<div class="trigger button">Trigger</div>
```

The event handler can be bound to the form:

```
$('.target').submit(function() {
  $(this).log('Submit event was triggered.');
});
```

Now when the form is submitted, the message is displayed. This happens prior to the actual submission, so we can cancel the submit action by calling `.preventDefault()` on the event or by returning `false` from our handler. We can trigger the event manually when the button is clicked:

```
$('.trigger').click(function() {
  $('.target').submit();
});
```

After this code executes, clicking the **Trigger** button will also display the message. In addition, the default submit action on the form will be fired, so the form will be submitted.

Keyboard Events

These events are triggered by the keys on the keyboard.

.keydown()

Binds an event handler to the keydown JavaScript event, or triggers that event on an element.

```
.keydown(handler)
```

```
.keydown()
```

Parameters (First Version)

- handler: A function to execute each time the event is triggered

Return Value

The jQuery object, for chaining purposes.

Description

This handler is a shortcut for `.bind('keydown', handler)` in the first variation, and `.trigger('keydown')` in the second.

The `keydown` event is sent to an element when the user first presses a key on the keyboard. It can be attached to any element, but the event is only sent to the element that has the focus. Focusable elements can vary between browsers, but form elements can always get focus so are reasonable candidates for this event type.

For example, consider the HTML:

```
<form>
  <input class="target" type="text" />
</form>
<div class="trigger button">Trigger</div>
```

The event handler can be bound to the input field:

```
$('.target').keydown(function() {
  $(this).log('Keydown event was triggered.');
});
```

Now when the insertion point is inside the field and a key is pressed, the message is displayed. We can trigger the event manually when the button is clicked:

```
$('.trigger').click(function() {
  $('.target').keydown();
});
```

After this code executes, clicking the **Triggers** button will also display the message.

If key presses anywhere need to be caught (for example, to implement global shortcut keys on a page), it is useful to attach this behavior to the `document` object. Because of event bubbling, all key presses will make their way up the DOM to the `document` object unless explicitly stopped.

To determine which key was pressed, we can examine the event object that is passed to the handler function. The `.keyCode` attribute typically holds this information, but in some older browsers `.which` stores the key code. JavaScript's `String` object has a `.fromCharCode()` method that can be used to convert this numeric code into a string containing the character for further processing.

The `fix_events.js` plug-in further standardizes the event object across different browsers. With this plug-in, we can use `.which` in all browsers to retrieve the key code.

.keypress()

Binds an event handler to the keypress JavaScript event, or triggers that event on an element.

```
.keypress(handler)
```
```
.keypress()
```

Parameters (First Version)

- handler: A function to execute each time the event is triggered

Return Value

The jQuery object, for chaining purposes.

Description

This handler is a shortcut for `.bind('keypress', handler)` in the first variation, and `.trigger('keypress')` in the second.

The `keypress` event is sent to an element when the browser registers keyboard input. This is similar to the `keydown` event, except in the case of key repeats. If the user presses and holds a key, a `keydown` event is triggered once, but separate `keypress` events are triggered for each inserted character. In addition, modifier keys (such as *Shift*) cause `keydown` events but not `keypress` events.

A `keypress` event handler can be attached to any element, but the event is only sent to the element that has the focus. Focusable elements can vary between browsers, but form elements can always get focus so are reasonable candidates for this event type.

For example, consider the HTML:

```
<form>
  <input class="target" type="text" />
</form>
<div class="trigger button">Trigger</div>
```

The event handler can be bound to the input field:

```
$('.target').keypress(function() {
  $(this).log('Keypress event was triggered.');
});
```

Now when the insertion point is inside the field and a key is pressed, the message is displayed. The message repeats if the key is held down. We can trigger the event manually when the button is clicked:

```
$('.trigger').click(function() {
  $('.target').keypress();
});
```

After this code executes, clicks on the **Trigger** button will also display the message.

If key presses anywhere need to be caught (for example, to implement global shortcut keys on a page), it is useful to attach this behavior to the document object. All key presses will make their way up the DOM to the document object unless explicitly stopped because of event bubbling.

To determine which key was pressed, we can examine the event object that is passed to the handler function. The .keyCode attribute typically holds this information, but in some older browsers .which stores the key code. JavaScript's String object has a .fromCharCode() method that can be used to convert this numeric code into a string containing the character for further processing.

Note that keydown and keyup provide a code indicating which key is pressed, while keypress indicates which character was entered. For example, a lowercase "a" will be reported as 65 by keydown and keyup, but as 97 by keypress. An uppercase "A" is reported as 97 by all events. This can be the primary motivator for deciding which event type to use.

.keyup()

> Binds an event handler to the keyup JavaScript event, or triggers that event on an element.
>
> .keyup(handler)
>
> .keyup()

Parameters (First Version)
- handler: A function to execute each time the event is triggered

Return Value
The jQuery object, for chaining purposes.

Description
This handler is a shortcut for .bind('keyup', handler) in the first variation, and .trigger('keyup') in the second.

The `keyup` event is sent to an element when the user releases a key on the keyboard. It can be attached to any element, but the event is only sent to the element that has the focus. Focusable elements can vary between browsers, but form elements can always get focus so are reasonable candidates for this event type.

For example, consider the HTML:

```
<form>
  <input class="target" type="text" />
</form>
<div class="trigger button">Trigger</div>
```

The event handler can be bound to the input field:

```
$('.target').keyup(function() {
  $(this).log('Keyup event was triggered.');
});
```

Now when the insertion point is inside the field and a key is pressed and released, the message is displayed. We can trigger the event manually when the button is clicked:

```
$('.trigger').click(function() {
  $('.target').keyup();
});
```

After this code executes, clicking the **Trigger** button will also display the message.

If key presses anywhere need to be caught (for example, to implement global shortcut keys on a page), it is useful to attach this behavior to the `document` object. All key presses will make their way up the DOM to the `document` object unless explicitly stopped because of event bubbling.

To determine which key was pressed, we can examine the event object that is passed to the handler function. The `.keyCode` attribute typically holds this information, but in some older browsers `.which` stores the key code. JavaScript's `String` object has a `.fromCharCode()` method that can be used to convert this numeric code into a string containing the character for further processing.

Browser Events

These events are related to the entire browser window.

.resize()

> Binds an event handler to the resize JavaScript event, or triggers that event on an element.
>
> ```
> .resize(handler)
> .resize()
> ```

Parameters (First Version)

- handler: A function to execute each time the event is triggered

Return Value

The jQuery object, for chaining purposes.

Description

This handler is a shortcut for `.bind('resize', handler)` in the first variation, and `.trigger('resize')` in the second.

The `resize` event is sent to the `window` element when the size of the browser window changes:

```
$(window).resize(function() {
  alert('Resize event was triggered.');
});
```

Now whenever the browser window's size is changed, the message is displayed.

The code in a `resize` handler should never rely on the number of times the handler is called. Depending on implementation, `resize` events can be sent continuously as the resizing is in progress (typical behavior in Internet Explorer), or only once at the end of the resize operation (typical behavior in FireFox).

.scroll()

> Binds an event handler to the scroll JavaScript event, or triggers that event on an element.
>
> ```
> .scroll(handler)
> .scroll()
> ```

Parameters (First Version)

- handler: A function to execute each time the event is triggered

Return Value

The jQuery object, for chaining purposes.

Description

This handler is a shortcut for `.bind('scroll', handler)` in the first variation, and `.trigger('scroll')` in the second.

The `scroll` event is sent to an element when the user scrolls to a different place in the element. It applies not only to `window` objects, but also to scrollable frames and elements with the `overflow: scroll` CSS property.

For example, consider the HTML:

```
<div class="target" style="overflow: scroll; width: 200px;
                                    height: 100px;">
  Lorem ipsum dolor sit amet, consectetur adipisicing elit, sed do
  eiusmod tempor incididunt ut labore et dolore magna aliqua. Ut enim
  ad minim veniam, quis nostrud exercitation ullamco laboris nisi ut
  aliquip ex ea commodo consequat. Duis aute irure dolor in
  reprehenderit in voluptate velit esse cillum dolore eu fugiat nulla
  pariatur. Excepteur sint occaecat cupidatat non proident, sunt in
  culpa qui officia deserunt mollit anim id est laborum.
</div>
<div class="trigger button">Trigger</div>
```

The style definition is present to make the target element small enough to be scrollable. The `scroll` event handler can be bound to this element:

```
$('.target').scroll(function() {
  $(this).log('Scroll event was triggered.');
});
```

Now when the user scrolls the text up or down, the message is displayed. We can trigger the event manually when the button is clicked:

```
$('.trigger').click(function() {
  $('.target').scroll();
});
```

After this code executes, clicking the **Trigger** button will also display the message.

A `scroll` event is sent whenever the element's scroll position changes, regardless of the cause. A mouse click or drag on the scroll bar, dragging inside the element, pressing the arrow keys, or using the mouse scroll wheel could cause this event.

6
Effect Methods

It's got style, it's got class
— Devo,
"Uncontrollable Urge"

In this chapter, we'll closely examine each of the effect methods, revealing all of the mechanisms jQuery has for providing visual feedback to the user.

Pre-Packaged Effects

These methods allow us to quickly apply commonly used effects with a minimum configuration.

.show()

Displays the matched elements.

```
.show([speed] [, callback])
```

Parameters

- speed (optional): A string or number determining how long the animation will run
- callback (optional): A function to call once the animation is complete

Return Value

The jQuery object, for chaining purposes.

Description

With no parameters, the `.show()` method is the simplest way to display an element:

```
$('.target').show();
```

The matched elements will be revealed immediately, with no animation. This is roughly equivalent to calling `.css('display', 'block')`, except that the `display` property is restored to whatever it was initially. If an element is given a `display` value of `inline`, then it is hidden and shown, it will once again be displayed `inline`.

When a speed is provided, `.show()` becomes an animation method. The `.show()` method animates the width, height, and opacity of the matched elements simultaneously.

Speeds are given in millisecond durations of the animation; higher values indicate slower animations, *not* faster ones. The strings `fast`, `normal`, and `slow` can be supplied to indicate speed values of `200`, `400`, and `600` respectively. If the speed parameter is omitted, `normal` is assumed.

If supplied, the callback is fired once the animation is complete. This can be useful for stringing different animations together in sequence. The callback is not sent any arguments, but `this` is set to the DOM element being animated. The callback is executed once per matched element, *not* once for the animation as a whole.

We can animate any element, such as a simple `<div>` containing an image:

```
<div class="content">
  <div class="trigger button">Trigger</div>
  <div class="target"><img src="hat.gif" width="80" height="54"
                                              alt="Hat" /></div>
  <div class="log"></div>
</div>
```

With the element initially hidden, we can show it slowly:

```
$('.trigger').click(function() {
  $('.target').show('slow', function() {
    $(this).log('Effect complete.');
  });
});
```

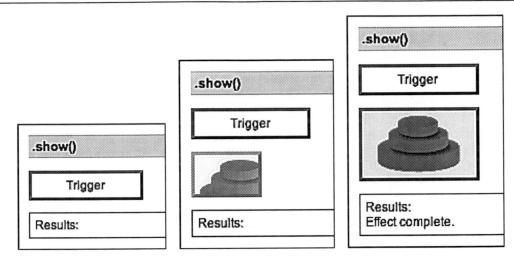

.hide()

Hides the matched elements.

```
.hide([speed][, callback])
```

Parameters

- speed (optional): A string or number determining how long the animation will run
- callback (optional): A function to call once the animation is complete

Return Value

The jQuery object, for chaining purposes.

Description

With no parameters, the `.hide()` method is the simplest way to hide an element:

```
$('.target').hide();
```

The matched elements will be hidden immediately, with no animation. This is roughly equivalent to calling `.css('display', 'none')`, except that the value of the display property is saved as another property of the element so that `display` can later be restored to its initial value. If an element is given a `display` value as `inline`, then it is hidden and shown, it will once again be displayed `inline`.

When a speed is provided, `.hide()` becomes an animation method. The `.hide()` method animates the width, height, and opacity of the matched elements simultaneously.

Speeds are given in millisecond durations of the animation; higher values indicate slower animations, *not* faster ones. The strings `fast`, `normal`, and `slow` can be supplied to indicate speed values of `200`, `400`, and `600` respectively. If the speed parameter is omitted, `normal` is assumed.

If supplied, the callback is fired once the animation is complete. This can be useful for stringing different animations together in sequence. The callback is not sent any arguments, but `this` is set to the DOM element being animated. The callback is executed once per matched element, not once for the animation as a whole.

We can animate any element, such as a simple `<div>` containing an image:

```
<div class="content">
  <div class="trigger button">Trigger</div>
  <div class="target"><img src="hat.gif" width="80" height="54"
                                          alt="Hat" /></div>
  <div class="log"></div>
</div>
```

With the element initially displayed, we can hide it slowly:

```
$('.trigger').click(function() {
  $('.target').hide('slow', function() {
    $(this).log('Effect complete.');
  });
});
```

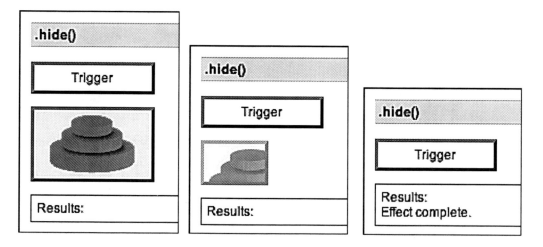

.toggle()

Displays or hides the matched elements.

```
.toggle([speed] [, callback])
```

Parameters

- speed (optional): A string or number determining how long the animation will run
- callback (optional): A function to call once the animation is complete

Return Value

The jQuery object, for chaining purposes.

Description

With no parameters, the .toggle() method simply toggles the visibility of elements:

```
$('.target').toggle();
```

The matched elements will be revealed or hidden immediately, with no animation. If the element is initially displayed, it will be hidden; if hidden, it will be shown. The display property is saved and restored as needed. If an element is given a display value of inline, then it is hidden and shown, it will once again be displayed inline.

When a speed is provided, .toggle() becomes an animation method. The .toggle() method animates the width, height, and opacity of the matched elements simultaneously.

Speeds are given in millisecond durations of the animation; higher values indicate slower animations, *not* faster ones. The strings fast, normal, and slow can be supplied to indicate speed values of 200, 400, and 600 respectively. If the speed parameter is omitted, normal is assumed.

If supplied, the callback is fired once the animation is complete. This can be useful for stringing different animations together in sequence. The callback is not sent any arguments, but this is set to the DOM element being animated. The callback is executed once per matched element, not once for the animation as a whole.

We can animate any element, such as a simple <div> containing an image:

```
<div class="content">
  <div class="trigger button">Trigger</div>
  <div class="target"><img src="hat.gif" width="80" height="54"
                                          alt="Hat" /></div>
  <div class="log"></div>
</div>
```

With the element initially displayed, we can hide and show it slowly:

```
$('.trigger').click(function() {
  $('.target').toggle('slow', function() {
    $(this).log('Effect complete.');
  });
});
```

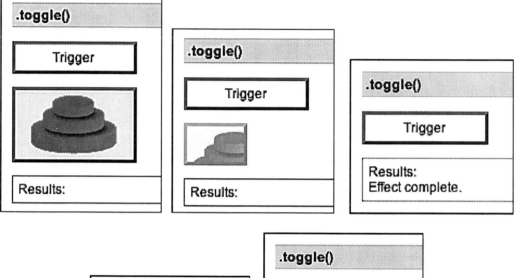

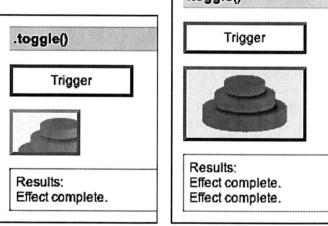

.slideDown()

Displays the matched elements with a sliding motion.

```
.slideDown([speed] [, callback])
```

Parameters

- speed (optional): A string or number determining how long the animation will run
- callback (optional): A function to call once the animation is complete

Return Value

The jQuery object, for chaining purposes.

Description

The `.slideDown()` method animates the height of the matched elements. This causes lower parts of the page to slide down, making way for the revealed items.

Speeds are given in millisecond durations of the animation; higher values indicate slower animations, *not* faster ones. The strings `fast`, `normal`, and `slow` can be supplied to indicate speed values of `200`, `400`, and `600` respectively. If the speed parameter is omitted, `normal` is assumed.

If supplied, the callback is fired once the animation is complete. This can be useful for stringing different animations together in sequence. The callback is not sent any arguments, but `this` is set to the DOM element being animated. The callback is executed once per matched element, not once for the animation as a whole.

We can animate any element, such as a simple `<div>` containing an image:

```
<div class="content">
  <div class="trigger button">Trigger</div>
  <div class="target"><img src="hat.gif" width="80" height="54"
                                          alt="Hat" /></div>
  <div class="log"></div>
</div>
```

With the element initially hidden, we can show it slowly:

```
$('.trigger').click(function() {
  $('.target').slideDown('slow', function() {
    $(this).log('Effect complete.');
  });
});
```

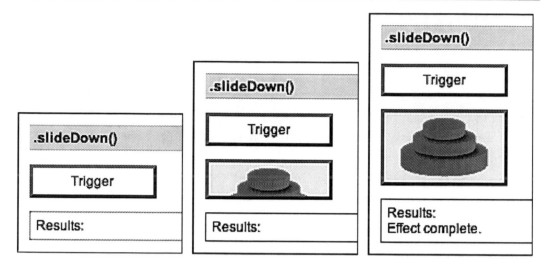

.slideUp()

Hides the matched elements with a sliding motion.

```
.slideUp([speed] [, callback])
```

Parameters

- speed (optional): A string or number determining how long the animation will run
- callback (optional): A function to call once the animation is complete

Return Value

The jQuery object, for chaining purposes.

Description

The .slideUp() method animates the height of the matched elements. This causes lower parts of the page to slide up, appearing to conceal the items.

Speeds are given in millisecond durations of the animation; higher values indicate slower animations, *not* faster ones. The strings fast, normal, and slow can be supplied to indicate speed values of 200, 400, and 600 respectively. If the speed parameter is omitted, normal is assumed.

If supplied, the callback is fired once the animation is complete. This can be useful for stringing different animations together in sequence. The callback is not sent any arguments, but `this` is set to the DOM element being animated. The callback is executed once per matched element, not once for the animation as a whole.

We can animate any element, such as a simple `<div>` containing an image:

```
<div class="content">
  <div class="trigger button">Trigger</div>
  <div class="target"><img src="hat.gif" width="80" height="54"
                                       alt="Hat" /></div>
  <div class="log"></div>
</div>
```

With the element initially visible, we can hide it slowly:

```
$('.trigger').click(function() {
  $('.target').slideUp('slow', function() {
    $(this).log('Effect complete.');
  });
});
```

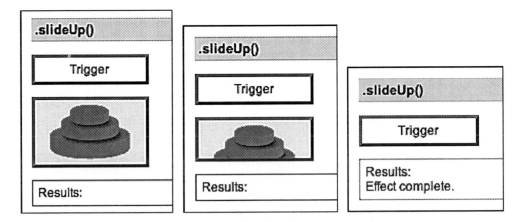

.slideToggle()

> Displays or hides the matched elements with a sliding motion.
>
> `.slideToggle([speed] [, callback])`

Parameters

- speed (optional): A string or number determining how long the animation will run

- callback (optional): A function to call once the animation is complete

Return Value

The jQuery object, for chaining purposes.

Description

The .slideToggle() method animates the height of the matched elements. This causes lower parts of the page to slide up or down, appearing to conceal or reveal the items.

Speeds are given in millisecond durations of the animation; higher values indicate slower animations, *not* faster ones. The strings fast, normal, and slow can be supplied to indicate speed values of 200, 400, and 600 respectively. If the speed parameter is omitted, normal is assumed.

If supplied, the callback is fired once the animation is complete. This can be useful for stringing different animations together in sequence. The callback is not sent any arguments, but this is set to the DOM element being animated. The callback is executed once per matched element, not once for the animation as a whole.

We can animate any element, such as a simple <div> containing an image:

```
<div class="content">
  <div class="trigger button">Trigger</div>
  <div class="target"><img src="hat.gif" width="80" height="54"
                                          alt="Hat" /></div>
  <div class="log"></div>
</div>
```

With the element initially displayed, we can hide and show it slowly:

```
$('.trigger').click(function() {
  $('.target').slideToggle('slow', function() {
    $(this).log('Effect complete.');
  });
});
```

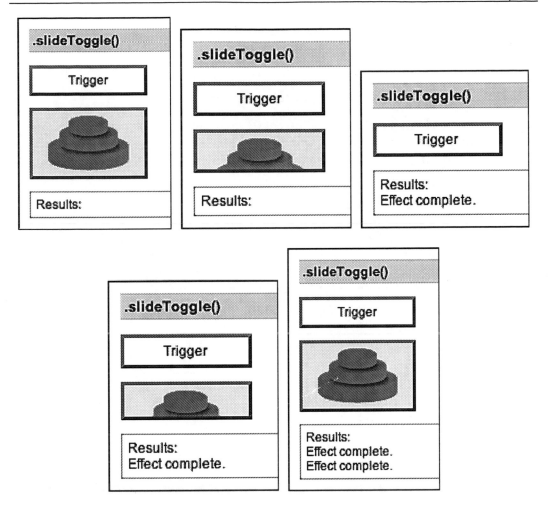

.fadeIn()

Displays the matched elements by fading them to opaque.

```
.fadeIn([speed] [, callback])
```

Parameters

- speed (optional): A string or number determining how long the animation will run
- callback (optional): A function to call once the animation is complete

Return Value

The jQuery object, for chaining purposes.

Description

The `.fadeIn()` method animates the opacity of the matched elements.

Speeds are given in millisecond durations of the animation; higher values indicate slower animations, *not* faster ones. The strings `fast`, `normal`, and `slow` can be supplied to indicate speed values of `200`, `400`, and `600` respectively. If the speed parameter is omitted, `normal` is assumed.

If supplied, the callback is fired once the animation is complete. This can be useful for stringing different animations together in sequence. The callback is not sent any arguments, but `this` is set to the DOM element being animated. The callback is executed once per matched element, *not* once for the animation as a whole.

We can animate any element, such as a simple `<div>` containing an image:

```
<div class="content">
  <div class="trigger button">Trigger</div>
  <div class="target"><img src="hat.gif" width="80" height="54"
                                         alt="Hat" /></div>
  <div class="log"></div>
</div>
```

With the element initially hidden, we can show it slowly:

```
$('.trigger').click(function() {
  $('.target').fadeIn('slow', function() {
    $(this).log('Effect complete.');
  });
});
```

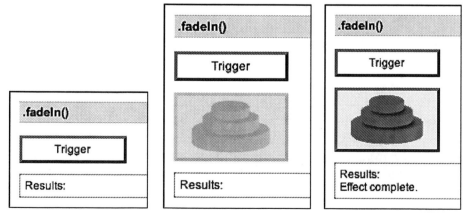

.fadeOut()

Hides the matched elements by fading them to transparent.

```
.fadeOut([speed] [, callback])
```

Parameters

- speed (optional): A string or number determining how long the animation will run
- callback (optional): A function to call once the animation is complete

Return Value

The jQuery object, for chaining purposes.

Description

The .fadeOut() method animates the opacity of the matched elements.

Speeds are given in millisecond durations of the animation; higher values indicate slower animations, *not* faster ones. The strings fast, normal, and slow can be supplied to indicate speed values of 200, 400, and 600 respectively. If the speed parameter is omitted, normal is assumed.

If supplied, the callback is fired once the animation is complete. This can be useful for stringing different animations together in sequence. The callback is not sent any arguments, but this is set to the DOM element being animated. The callback is executed once per matched element, *not* once for the animation as a whole.

We can animate any element, such as a simple <div> containing an image:

```
<div class="content">
  <div class="trigger button">Trigger</div>
  <div class="target"><img src="hat.gif" width="80" height="54"
                                          alt="Hat" /></div>
  <div class="log"></div>
</div>
```

With the element initially displayed, we can hide it slowly:

```
$('.trigger').click(function() {
  $('.target').fadeOut('slow', function() {
    $(this).log('Effect complete.');
  });
});
```

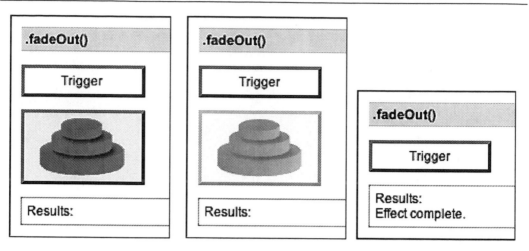

.fadeTo()

Adjusts the opacity of the matched elements.

```
.fadeTo(speed, opacity[, callback])
```

Parameters

- speed: A string or number determining how long the animation will run
- opacity: A number between 0 and 1 denoting the target opacity
- callback: (optional): A function to call once the animation is complete

Return Value

The jQuery object, for chaining purposes.

Description

The .fadeTo() method animates the opacity of the matched elements.

Speeds are given in millisecond durations of the animation; higher values indicate slower animations, *not* faster ones. The strings fast, normal, and slow can be supplied to indicate speed values of 200, 400, and 600 respectively. Unlike the other effect methods, .fadeTo() requires that the speed should be explicitly specified.

If supplied, the callback is fired once the animation is complete. This can be useful for stringing different animations together in sequence. The callback is not sent any arguments, but this is set to the DOM element being animated. The callback is executed once per matched element, *not* once for the animation as a whole.

We can animate any element, such as a simple `<div>` containing an image:

```
<div class="content">
  <div class="trigger button">Trigger</div>
  <div class="target"><img src="hat.gif" width="80" height="54"
                                        alt="Hat" /></div>
  <div class="log"></div>
</div>
```

With the element initially displayed, we can dim it slowly:

```
$('.trigger').click(function() {
  $('.target').fadeTo('slow', 0.5, function() {
    $(this).log('Effect complete.');
  });
});
```

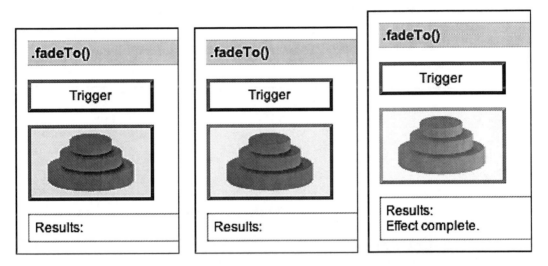

With *speed* set to 0, this method just changes the opacity CSS property, so
`.fadeTo(0, opacity)` is the same as `.css('opacity', opacity)`.

 In jQuery versions prior to 1.1.3, `.fadeTo()` sets the `display` property of the element to `block`. This can lead to strange layout renderings when used with non-block items such as table rows and inline elements. As of jQuery 1.1.3, fades can be used safely for these elements.

Customized Effects

This section describes how to create effects that are not provided out-of-the-box by jQuery.

.animate()

Performs a custom animation of a set of CSS properties.

.animate(properties[, speed][, easing][, callback])

Parameters

- properties: A map of CSS properties that the animation will move toward
- speed (optional): A string or number determining how long the animation will run
- easing (optional): A string indicating which easing function to use for the transition
- callback (optional): A function to call once the animation is complete

Return Value

The jQuery object, for chaining purposes.

Description

The .animate() method allows us to create animation effects on any numeric CSS property. The only required parameter is a map of CSS properties. This map is similar to the one that can be sent to the .css() method, except that the range of properties is more restrictive.

All animated properties are treated as a number of pixels. If the property was initially specified in different units, such as ems or percent, this can produce strange results.

In addition to numeric values, each property can take the strings show, hide, and toggle. These shortcuts allow for custom hiding and showing animations that take into account the display type of the element.

Speeds are given in millisecond durations of the animation; higher values indicate slower animations, *not* faster ones. The strings fast, normal, and slow can be supplied to indicate speed values of 200, 400, and 600 respectively. If the speed parameter is omitted, normal is assumed.

If supplied, the callback is fired once the animation is complete. This can be useful for stringing different animations together in sequence. The callback is not sent any arguments, but `this` is set to the DOM element being animated. The callback is executed once per matched element, *not* once for the animation as a whole.

We can animate any element, such as a simple `<div>` containing an image:

```
<div class="content">
  <div class="trigger button">Trigger</div>
  <div class="target"><img src="hat.gif" width="80" height="54"
                                         alt="Hat" /></div>
  <div class="log"></div>
</div>
```

We can animate several properties at once:

```
$('.trigger').click(function() {
  $('.target').animate({
    'width': 300,
    'left': 100,
    'opacity': 0.25
  }, 'slow', function() {
    $(this).log('Effect complete.');
  });
});
```

The `position` attribute of the element must not be `fixed` if we wish to animate the `left` property as we do in the example.

> A more sophisticated version of the `.animate()` method can be found in the *Interface* plug-in. It handles some non-numeric styles such as colors, and also handles animating classes rather than individual attributes.

The remaining parameter of `.animate()` is a string naming an easing function to use. An easing function specifies the speed at which the animation progresses at different points within the animation. The only easing implementation in the jQuery library is the default, `linear`. More easing functions are available with the use of plug-ins, such as Interface.

7
AJAX Methods

She's out of sync
She entered through the exit
And never stopped to think
　　　　　　— Devo
　　　"Out of Sync"

The AJAX capabilities in jQuery help us to load data from the server without a browser page refresh. In this chapter, we'll examine each of the available AJAX methods and functions. We'll see various ways of initiating an AJAX request, as well as several methods that can observe the requests that are in progress at any time.

Low-Level Interface

These methods can be used to make arbitrary AJAX requests.

$.ajax()

> Perform an asynchronous HTTP (AJAX) request.
>
> ```
> $.ajax(settings)
> ```

Parameters

- settings: A map of options for the request can contain the following items:

    ◦ url: A string containing the URL to which the request is sent.

    ◦ type (optional): A string defining the HTTP method to use for the request (GET or POST). The default value is GET.

    ◦ dataType (optional): A string defining the type of data expected back from the server (xml, html, json, or script).

    ◦ ifModified (optional): A Boolean indicating whether the server should check if the page is modified before responding to the request.

    ◦ timeout (optional): Number of milliseconds after which the request will time out in failure.

    ◦ global (optional): A Boolean indicating whether global AJAX event handlers will be triggered by this request. The default value is true.

    ◦ beforeSend (optional): A callback function that is executed before the request is sent.

    ◦ error (optional): A callback function that is executed if the request fails.

    ◦ success (optional): A callback function that is executed if the request succeeds.

    ◦ complete (optional): A callback function that executes whenever the request finishes.

    ◦ data (optional): A map or string that is sent to the server with the request.

    ◦ processData (optional): A Boolean indicating whether to convert the submitted data from an object form into a query-string form. The default value is true.

    ◦ contentType (optional): A string containing a MIME content type to set for the request. The default value is application/x-www-form-urlencoded.

    ◦ async (optional): A Boolean indicating whether to perform the request asynchronously. The default value is true.

Return Value

The XMLHttpRequest object that was created.

Description

The $.ajax() function underlies all AJAX requests sent by jQuery. This function is seldom directly called as several higher-level alternatives like $.post() and .load() are available and are easier to use. If less common options are required, though, $.ajax() can be used for more flexibility.

At its simplest, the $.ajax() function must atleast specify a URL from which the data is to be loaded:

```
$.ajax({
  url: 'ajax/test.html',
});
```

 Even this sole required parameter can be made optional by setting a default using the $.ajaxSetup() function.

This example, using the only required option, loads the contents of the specified URL, but does nothing with the result. To use the result, we can implement one of the callback functions. The beforeSend, error, success, and complete options take callback functions that are invoked at the appropriate times:

- beforeSend: called before the request is sent; the XMLHttpRequest object is passed as a parameter to it.
- error: called if the request fails. The XMLHttpRequest object is passed as a parameter as a string indicating the error type, and an exception object if applicable.
- success: called if the request succeeds. The returned data is passed as the parameter to it.
- complete: called when the request finishes, whether in failure or success. The XMLHttpRequest object as well as a string containing the success or error code are passed as a parameters to it.

To make use of the returned HTML, we can implement a success handler:

```
$.ajax({
  url: 'ajax/test.html',
  success: function(data) {
    $('.result').html(data);
    $().log('Load was performed.');
  },
});
```

Such a simple example would generally be better served by using .load() or
$.get().

The $.ajax() function relies on the server to provide information about the
retrieved data. If the server reports the return data as XML, the result can be
traversed using normal XML methods or jQuery's selectors. If another type is
detected, such as HTML in the example above, the data is treated as text.

Different data handling can be achieved by using the dataType option. Besides plain
xml, the dataType can be html, json, or script. If html is specified, any embedded
JavaScript inside the retrieved data is executed before the HTML is returned as a
string. Similarly, script will execute the JavaScript that is pulled back from the
server and return the script itself as textual data. The json option uses eval() to
parse the fetched data file as a JavaScript object, and return the constructed object as
the result data.

 We must ensure that the MIME type that is reported by the web server
matches our choice of dataType. In particular, xml must be declared by
the server as text/xml for consistent results.

By default, AJAX requests are sent using the GET HTTP method. If the POST method
is required, the method can be specified by setting a value for the type option. This
option affects how the contents of the data option are sent to the server.

The data option can contain either a query string of the form
key1=value1&key2=value2, or a map of the form {key1: 'value1', key2:
'value2'}. If the latter form is used, the data is converted into a query string
before it is sent. This processing can be prevented by setting processData to false.
The processing might be undesirable if we wish to send an XML object to the
server; in this case, we would also want to change the contentType option from
application/x-www-form-urlencoded to a more appropriate MIME type.

The remaining options — ifModified, timeout, global, and async — are rarely
required. For information on ifModified, please refer to the $.getIfModified()
function. Request timeouts can usually be set as a global default using
$.ajaxSetup() rather than for specific requests with the timeout option. The
global option prevents registered handlers that use .ajaxSend(), .ajaxError(),
or similar methods from firing when triggered by this request. This can be useful to,
for example, suppress a loading indicator that we implemented with .ajaxSend() if
the requests are frequent and brief. Lastly, the default value for async option is true,
indicating that the code execution can be continued after the request is made.
Setting this option to false is strongly discouraged as it can cause the browser to
become unresponsive.

> Rather than making requests synchronous using this option, better results can be achieved using the *blockUI* plug-in..

The $.ajax() function returns the XMLHttpRequest object that it creates. This can generally be discarded, but it does provide a lower-level interface for observing and manipulating the request. In particular, calling .abort() on the object will halt the request before it completes.

$.ajaxSetup()

Sets default values for future AJAX requests.

```
$.ajaxSetup(settings)
```

Parameters

- settings: A map of options for future requests. Same possible items as in $.ajax().

Return Value

None.

Description

For details on the settings available for $.ajaxSetup(), please refert to $.ajax(). All subsequent AJAX calls using any function will use the new settings, unless overridden by the individual calls, until the next invocation of $.ajaxSetup().

For example, we could set a default value for the URL parameter before pinging the server repeatedly:

```
$.ajaxSetup({
  url: 'ping.php',
});
```

Now each time an AJAX request is made, this URL will be used automatically:

```
$.ajax({});
$.ajax({
  data: {'date': Date()},
});
```

Shorthand Methods

These methods perform the more common types of AJAX requests in less code.

$.get()

Loads data from the server using a GET HTTP request.

```
$.get(url[, data][, success])
```

Parameters

- url: A string containing the URL to which the request is sent
- data: (optional): A map of data that is sent with the request
- success: (optional): A function that is executed if the request succeeds

Return Value

The XMLHttpRequest object that was created.

Description

This is a shorthand AJAX function, which is equivalent to:

```
$.ajax({
  url: url,
  data: data,
  success: success
});
```

The callback is passed the returned data, which will be an XML root element or a text string depending on the MIME type of the response.

Most implementations will specify a success handler:

```
$.get('ajax/test.html', function(data) {
  $('.result').html(data);
  $().log('Load was performed.');
});
```

This example fetches the requested HTML snippet and inserts it on the page.

$.getIfModified()

> Loads data from the server using a GET HTTP request if it has changed since the last request.
>
> $.getIfModified(url[, data][, success])

Parameters

- url: A string containing the URL to which the request is sent
- data: (optional): A map of data that is sent with the request
- success: (optional): A function that is executed if the request succeeds

Return Value

The XMLHttpRequest object that was created.

Description

This is a shorthand AJAX function, which is equivalent to:

```
$.ajax({
  url: url,
  data: data,
  success: success,
  ifModified: true
});
```

The callback is passed the returned data, which will be an XML root element or a text string depending on the MIME type of the response.

Most implementations will specify a success handler:

```
$.getIfModified('ajax/test.html', function(data) {
  if (data) {
    $('.result').html(data);
  }
  $().log('Load was performed.');
});
```

This example fetches the requested HTML snippet and inserts it on the page.

When the AJAX request is sent, an If-Modified-Since HTTP header is added. Web servers are supposed to honor this and omit the data if the file is unchanged. This can be exploited to save bandwidth when refreshing data from within a page.

A response that the page is not modified is still treated as a success. In this case the callback will still be executed, but no data will be available. The callback should trap for this to avoid discarding previously-fetched data.

.load()

> Loads data from the server and places the returned HTML into the matched element.
>
> `.load(url[, data][, success])`

Parameters

- url: A string containing the URL to which the request is sent
- data (optional): A map of data that is sent with the request
- success (optional): A function that is executed if the request succeeds

Return Value

The jQuery object, for chaining purposes.

Description

This method is the simplest way to fetch data from the server. It is roughly equivalent to $.get(url, data, success) except that it is a method rather than a global function and it has an implicit callback function. When a successful response is detected, .load() sets the HTML contents of the matched element to the returned data. This means that most uses of the method can be quite simple:

```
$('.result').load('ajax/test.html');
```

The provided callback, if any, is executed after this post-processing has been performed:

```
$('.result').load('ajax/test.html', function() {
  $(this).log('Load was performed.');
});
```

The POST method is used if data is provided; otherwise, GET is assumed.

 The event handling suite also has a method named .load(). Which one is fired depends on the set of arguments passed.

.loadIfModified()

Loads data from the server, if it has changed since the last request, and places the returned HTML into the matched element.

```
.loadIfModified(url[, data][, success])
```

Parameters

- url: A string containing the URL to which the request is sent
- data: (optional): A map of data that is sent with the request
- success: (optional): A function that is executed if the request succeeds

Return Value

The jQuery object, for chaining purposes.

Description

This method is roughly equivalent to `$.getIfModified(url, data, success)` except that it is a method rather than a global function and it has an implicit callback function. When a successful response is detected, `.loadIfModified()` sets the HTML contents of the matched element to the returned data. This means that most uses of the method can be quite simple:

```
$('.result').loadIfModified('ajax/test.html');
```

The provided callback, if any, is executed after this post-processing has been performed:

```
$('.result').loadIfModified('ajax/test.html', function() {
  $(this).log('Load was performed.');
});
```

The POST method is used if data is provided; otherwise, GET is assumed.

For more information on how the modification date checking works, see `$.getIfModified()`

$.post()

Loads data from the server using a POST HTTP request.

```
$.post(url[, data][, success])
```

Parameters

- url: A string containing the URL to which the request is sent
- data: (optional): A map of data that is sent with the request
- success: (optional): A function that is executed if the request succeeds

Return Value

The XMLHttpRequest object that was created.

Description

This is a shorthand AJAX function, which is equivalent to:

```
$.ajax({
  type: 'POST',
  url: url,
  data: data,
  success: success
});
```

The callback is passed the returned data, which will be an XML root element or a text string depending on the MIME type of the response.

Most implementations will specify a success handler:

```
$.post('ajax/test.html', function(data) {
  $('.result').html(data);
  $().log('Load was performed.');
});
```

This example fetches the requested HTML snippet and inserts it on the page.

Pages fetched with POST are never cached, so the ifModified option has no effect on these requests.

$.getJSON()

Loads JSON-encoded data from the server using a GET HTTP request.

```
$.getJSON(url[, data][, success])
```

Parameters

- url: A string containing the URL to which the request is sent
- data: (optional): A map of data that is sent with the request
- success: (optional): A function that is executed if the request succeeds

Return Value

The XMLHttpRequest object that was created.

Description

This is a shorthand AJAX function, which is equivalent to:

```
$.ajax({
  url: url,
  dataType: 'json',
  data: data,
  success: success
});
```

The callback is passed the returned data, which will be a JavaScript object or array as defined by the JSON structure and parsed using the eval() function.

For details on the JSON format, see http://json.org/.

Most implementations will specify a success handler:

```
$.getJSON('ajax/test.json', function(data) {
  $('.result').html('<p>' + data.foo + '</p><p>' + data.baz[1]
                                                    + '</p>');
  $().log('Load was performed.');
});
```

This example, of course, relies on the structure of the JSON file:

```
{
    "foo": "The quick brown fox jumps over the lazy dog.",
    "bar": "How razorback-jumping frogs can level six piqued gymnasts!",
    "baz": [52, 97]
}
```

Using this structure, the example inserts the first string and second number from the file onto the page. If there is a syntax error in the JSON file, the request will usually fail silently; avoid frequent hand-editing of JSON data for this reason.

$.getScript()

Loads a JavaScript from the server using a GET HTTP request, and executes it.

```
$.getScript(url[, success])
```

Parameters

- url: A string containing the URL to which the request is sent
- success: (optional): A function that is executed if the request succeeds

Return Value

The XMLHttpRequest object that was created.

Descritpion

This is a shorthand AJAX function, which is equivalent to:

```
$.ajax({
  url: url,
  type: 'script',
  success: success
});
```

The callback is passed the returned JavaScript file. This is generally not useful as the script will already have run at this point.

The script is executed in the global context, so it can refer to other variables and use jQuery functions. Included scripts should have some impact on the current page:

```
$('.result').html('<p>Lorem ipsum dolor sit amet.</p>');
```

The script can then be included and run by referencing the file name:

```
$.getScript('ajax/test.js', function() {
  $().log('Load was performed.');
});
```

In Safari, the script is not guaranteed to execute before the success callback is invoked. Practically speaking, this means that the code in the callback should not call functions or reference variables defined in the external script without at least a small delay.

Global AJAX Event Handlers

These methods register handlers to be called when certain events take place for any AJAX request on the page.

.ajaxComplete()

Registers a handler to be called when AJAX requests complete.

```
.ajaxComplete(handler)
```

Parameters

- handler: The function to be invoked

Return Value

The jQuery object, for chaining purposes.

Description

Whenever an AJAX request completes, jQuery triggers the ajaxComplete event. All the handlers that have been registered with the .ajaxComplete() method are executed at this time.

To observe this method in action, we can set up a basic AJAX load request:

```
<div class="trigger button">Trigger</div>
<div class="result"></div>
<div class="log"></div>
```

We can attach our event handler to any element:

```
$('.log').ajaxComplete(function() {
  $(this).log('Triggered ajaxComplete handler.');
});
```

Now, we can make an AJAX request using any jQuery method:

```
$('.trigger').click(function() {
  $('.result').load('ajax/test.html');
});
```

When the user clicks the button and the AJAX request completes, the log message is displayed.

All ajaxComplete handlers are invoked, regardless of what AJAX request was completed. If we must differentiate between the requests, we can use the parameters passed to the handler. Each time an ajaxComplete handler is executed, it is passed the event object, the XMLHttpRequest object, and the settings object that was used in the creation of the request. For example, we can restrict our callback to only handling events dealing with a particular URL:

```
$('.log').ajaxComplete(function(e, xhr, settings) {
  if (settings.url == 'ajax/test.html') {
    $(this).log('Triggered ajaxComplete handler for
                                    "ajax/test.html".');
  }
});
```

.ajaxError()

Registers a handler to be called when AJAX requests complete with an error.

```
.ajaxError(handler)
```

Parameters

- handler: The function to be invoked

Return Value

The jQuery object, for chaining purposes.

Description

Whenever an AJAX request completes with an error, jQuery triggers the `ajaxError` event. All the handlers that have been registered with the `.ajaxError()` method are executed at this time.

To observe this method in action, we can set up a basic AJAX load request:

```
<div class="trigger button">Trigger</div>
<div class="result"></div>
<div class="log"></div>
```

We can attach our event handler to any element:

```
$('.log').ajaxError(function() {
  $(this).log('Triggered ajaxError handler.');
});
```

Now, we can make an AJAX request using any jQuery method:

```
$('.trigger').click(function() {
  $('.result').load('ajax/missing.html');
});
```

When the user clicks the button and the AJAX request fails, because the requested file is missing, the log message is displayed.

All `ajaxError` handlers are invoked, regardless of what AJAX request was completed. If we must differentiate between the requests, we can use the parameters passed to the handler. Each time an `ajaxError` handler is executed, it is passed the event object, the `XMLHttpRequest` object, and the settings object that was used in the creation of the request. If the request failed because JavaScript raised an exception, the exception object is passed to the handler as a fourth parameter. For example, we can restrict our callback to only handling events dealing with a particular URL:

```
$('.log').ajaxError(function(e, xhr, settings, exception) {
  if (settings.url == 'ajax/missing.html') {
    $(this).log('Triggered ajaxError handler for
                                  "ajax/missing.html".');
  }
});
```

.ajaxSend()

Registers a handler to be called when AJAX requests begins.

    .ajaxSend(handler)

Parameters
- handler: The function to be invoked

Return Value
The jQuery object, for chaining purposes.

Description
Whenever an AJAX request is about to be sent, jQuery triggers the `ajaxSend` event. All the handlers that have been registered with the `.ajaxSend()` method are executed at this instant of time.

To observe this method in action, we can set up a basic AJAX load request:

```
<div class="trigger button">Trigger</div>
<div class="result"></div>
<div class="log"></div>
```

We can attach our event handler to any element:

```
$('.log').ajaxSend(function() {
  $(this).log('Triggered ajaxSend handler.');
});
```

Now, we can make an AJAX request using any jQuery method:

```
$('.trigger').click(function() {
  $('.result').load('ajax/test.html');
});
```

When the user clicks the button and the AJAX request is about to begin, the log message is displayed.

All ajaxSend handlers are invoked, regardless of what AJAX request is to be sent. If we must differentiate between the requests, we can use the parameters passed to the handler. Each time an ajaxSend handler is executed, it is passed the event object, the XMLHttpRequest object, and the settings object that was used in the creation of the request. For example, we can restrict our callback to only handling events dealing with a particular URL:

```
$('.log').ajaxSend(function(e, xhr, settings) {
  if (settings.url == 'ajax/test.html') {
    $(this).log('Triggered ajaxSend handler for "ajax/test.html".');
  }
});
```

.ajaxStart()

Registers a handler to be called when the first AJAX request begins.

```
.ajaxStart(handler)
```

Parameters

- handler: The function to be invoked

Return Value

The jQuery object, for chaining purposes.

Description

Whenever an AJAX request is about to be sent, jQuery checks whether there are any other outstanding AJAX requests. If none are in progress, jQuery triggers the ajaxStart event. All the handlers that have been registered with the .ajaxStart() method are executed at this instant of time.

To observe this method in action, we can set up a basic AJAX load request:

```
<div class="trigger button">Trigger</div>
<div class="result"></div>
<div class="log"></div>
```

We can attach our event handler to any element:

```
$('.log').ajaxStart(function() {
  $(this).log('Triggered ajaxStart handler.');
});
```

Now, we can make an AJAX request using any jQuery method:

```
$('.trigger').click(function() {
  $('.result').load('ajax/test.html');
});
```

When the user clicks the button and the AJAX request is sent, the log message is displayed.

.ajaxStop()

> Registers a handler to be called when all AJAX requests have completed.
>
>   .ajaxStop(handler)

Parameters
- handler: The function to be invoked

Return Value
The jQuery object, for chaining purposes.

Description
Whenever an AJAX request completes, jQuery checks whether there are any other outstanding AJAX requests; if none are remaining, jQuery triggers the `ajaxStop` event. All the handlers that have been registered with the `.ajaxStop()` method are executed at this instant of time.

To observe this method in action, we can set up a basic AJAX load request:

```
<div class="trigger button">Trigger</div>
<div class="result"></div>
<div class="log"></div>
```

We can attach our event handler to any element:

```
$('.log').ajaxStop(function() {
  $(this).log('Triggered ajaxStop handler.');
});
```

Now, we can make an AJAX request using any jQuery method:

```
$('.trigger').click(function() {
  $('.result').load('ajax/test.html');
});
```

When the user clicks the button and the AJAX request completes, the log message is displayed.

 Because .ajaxStart(), .ajaxStop(), .ajaxSend(), ajaxError(), and .ajaxComplete() are implemented as a methods rather than global functions, we can use the keyword this as we do here to refer to the selected elements within the callback function.

.ajaxSuccess()

Registers a handler to be called when AJAX requests are successfully completed.

```
.ajaxSuccess(handler)
```

Parameters

- handler: The function to be invoked

Return Value

The jQuery object, for chaining purposes.

Description

Whenever an AJAX request is successfully completed, jQuery triggers the ajaxSuccess event. All the handlers that have been registered with the .ajaxSuccess() method are executed at this instant of time.

To observe this method in action, we can set up a basic AJAX load request:

```
<div class="trigger button">Trigger</div>
<div class="result"></div>
<div class="log"></div>
```

We can attach our event handler to any element:

```
$('.log').ajaxSuccess(function() {
  $(this).log('Triggered ajaxSuccess handler.');
});
```

Now, we can make an AJAX request using any jQuery method:

```
$('.trigger').click(function() {
  $('.result').load('ajax/test.html');
});
```

When the user clicks the button and the AJAX request successfully completes, the log message is displayed.

 Because .ajaxSuccess() is implemented as a method rather than a global function, we can use the this keyword as we do here to refer to the selected elements within the callback function.

All ajaxSuccess handlers are invoked, regardless of what AJAX request was completed. If we must differentiate between the requests, we can use the parameters passed to the handler. Each time an ajaxSuccess handler is executed, it is passed the event object, the XMLHttpRequest object, and the settings object that was used in the creation of the request. For example, we can restrict our callback only to handling events dealing with a particular URL:

```
$('.log').ajaxSuccess(function(e, xhr, settings) {
  if (settings.url == 'ajax/test.html') {
    $(this).log('Triggered ajaxSuccess handler for
                                    "ajax/test.html".');
  }
});
```

Helper Function

This function assists with common idioms encountered when performing AJAX tasks.

.serialize()

Encodes a set of form elements as a string for submission.

> .serialize(param)

Parameters

None.

Return Value

A string containing the serialized representation of the elements.

Description

The `.serialize()` method creates a text string in standard URL-encoded notation. It operates on a jQuery object representing a set of form elements. The form elements can be of several types:

```
<form>
  <div><input type="text" name="a" value="1" id="a" /></div>
  <div><input type="text" name="b" value="2" id="b" /></div>
  <div><input type="hidden" name="c" value="3" id="c" /></div>
  <div><textarea name="d" rows="8" cols="40">4</textarea></div>
  <div><select name="e">
    <option value="5" selected="selected">5</option>
    <option value="6">6</option>
    <option value="7">7</option>
  </select></div>
  <div><input type="checkbox" name="f" value="8" id="f" /></div>
  <div><input type="submit" name="g" value="Submit" id="g">
</form>
```

We can serialize all of these element types after selecting them:

```
$('form').submit(function() {
  $(this).log($('input, textarea, select').serialize());
  return false;
});
```

This produces a standard-looking query string:

```
a=1&b=2&c=3&f=8&g=Submit&d=4&e=5
```

The string is close to, but not exactly the same as, the one that would be produced by the browser during a normal form submission. The `.submit()` method uses the `.name` and `.value` properties of each element to create the string, so in cases where these properties do not reflect the actual form values, the string can be incorrect. For example, the checkbox in the example above always has a `.value` of 8, whether or not the box is checked.

For a more robust solution, the *form* plug-in is available. Its methods provide an encoding that matches the one provided by a browser.

8

Miscellaneous Methods

Freedom of choice is what you got
Freedom from choice is what you want
                            — Devo,
            "Freedom of Choice"

In the preceding chapters, we have examined many categories of jQuery methods. A few methods provided by the library have so far defied **categorization**, though. In this chapter, we will explore methods that can be used to abbreviate common JavaScript idioms.

Setup Methods

These functions are useful before the main code body begins.

$.browser

Contains information about the currently running browser.

    $.browser

Parameters

None.

Return Value

Boolean flags for each user agent possibility.

Description

The $.browser property allows us to detect which web browser is accessing the page, as reported by the browser itself. It contains flags for each of the four most prevalent browser classes—Internet Explorer, Mozilla, Safari, and Opera. The browsers can be tested independently:

```
$()
   .log('Safari: ' + $.browser.safari)
   .log('Opera: ' + $.browser.opera)
   .log('MSIE: ' + $.browser.msie)
   .log('Mozilla: ' + $.browser.mozilla);
```

When executed on a Firefox browser, the results are:

```
Safari: false
Opera: false
MSIE: false
Mozilla: true
```

This property is available immediately. It is therefore safe to use it to determine whether or not to call $(document).ready().

Because $.browser uses navigator.useragent to determine the platform, it is vulnerable to spoofing by the user. It is always best to avoid browser-specific code entirely where possible. In special cases where it needs to be written for different agents, the best alternative is to test for the presence of the JavaScript features you want to use. If this does not differentiate the clients well enough, the $.browser property can be used for further distinctions.

$.noConflict()

> Relinquishes jQuery's control of the $ variable.
>
> ```
> $.noConflict()
> ```

Parameters

None.

Return Value

The global jQuery object. This can be set to a variable to provide an alternative shortcut to $.

Description

Many JavaScript libraries use $ as a function or variable name, just as jQuery does. In jQuery's case, $ is just an alias for jQuery, so all functionality is available without using $. If we need to use another JavaScript library alongside jQuery, we can return control of $ back to the other library with a call to $.noConflict():

```
// Import other library
// Import jQuery
$.noConflict();
// Code that uses other library's $ can follow here.
```

This technique is especially effective in conjunction with the .ready() method's ability to alias the jQuery object, as within the .ready() we can use $ if we wish without fear of conflicts later:

```
// Import other library
// Import jQuery
$.noConflict();
jQuery(document).ready(function($) {
   // Code that uses jQuery's $ can follow here.
});
// Code that uses other library's $ can follow here.
```

DOM Element Methods

These methods help us to work with the DOM elements underlying each jQuery object.

.length

Returns the number of DOM elements matched by the jQuery object.

```
.length
```

Parameters

None.

Return Value

The number of elements matched.

Description

Suppose we had a simple unordered list on the page:

```
<ul>
  <li>foo</li>
  <li>bar</li>
</ul>
```

We can determine the number of list items by calling `.length`:

```
$().log('Length: ' + $('li').length);
```

.size()

> Returns the number of DOM elements matched by the jQuery object.
>
> `.size()`

Parameters

None.

Return Value

The number of elements matched.

Description

Suppose we had a simple unordered list on the page:

```
<ul>
  <li>foo</li>
  <li>bar</li>
</ul>
```

We can determine the number of list items by calling `.size()`:

```
$().log('Size: ' + $('li').size());
```

.get()

> Retrieves DOM elements matched by the jQuery object.
>
> `.get([index])`

Parameters

- index (optional): An integer indicating which element to retrieve

Return Value

A DOM element, or an array of DOM elements if the index is omitted.

Description

The `.get()` method grants us access to the DOM nodes underlying each jQuery object. Suppose we had a simple unordered list on the page:

```
<ul>
  <li>foo</li>
  <li>bar</li>
</ul>
```

With an index specified, `.get()` will retrieve a single element:

```
$().log('Get(0): ' + $('li').get(0));
```

Since the index is zero-based, the first list item is returned:

```
Get(0): [object HTMLLIElement]
```

Each jQuery object also masquerades as an array, so we can use the array dereferencing operator to get at the list item instead:

```
$().log('Get(0): ' + $('li')[0]);
```

Without a parameter, `.get()` returns all of the matched DOM nodes in a regular array:

```
$().log('Get(): ' + $('li').get());
```

In our example, this means that all list items are returned:

```
Get(): [object HTMLLIElement],[object HTMLLIElement]
```

.index()

Searches for a given DOM node from among the matched elements.

```
.index(node)
```

Parameters

- node: The DOM element to look for

Return Value

The position of the element within the jQuery object, or -1 if not found.

Description

The complementary operation to .get(), that accepts an index and returns a DOM node, .index() takes a DOM node and returns an index. Suppose we had a simple unordered list on the page:

```
<ul>
  <li>foo</li>
  <li>bar</li>
</ul>
```

If we retrieve one of the two list items, we can store it in a variable. Then .index() can search for this list item within the set of matched elements:

```
var listItem = $('li')[1];
$().log('Index: ' + $('li').index(listItem));
```

We get back the zero-based position of the list item:

```
Index: 1
```

Collection Manipulation

These helper functions manipulate arrays, maps, and strings.

.each()

Iterates over a collection, firing a callback function on each item.

```
.each(callback)
$.each(collection, callback)
```

Parameters (First Version)

- callback: A function to execute for each matched element

Return Value (First Version)

The jQuery object, for chaining purposes.

Parameters (Second Version)

- collection: An object or an array to iterate over
- callback: A function to execute for each item in the collection

Return Value (Second Version)

The collection.

Description

The `.each()` method and `$.each()` function are generic iterators designed to make concise and less error-prone looping constructs. They operate on a collection, and execute a callback function once for every item in that collection.

The first syntax listed above is a method of jQuery objects, and when called it iterates over the DOM elements that are part of the object. Each time the callback runs, it is passed the current loop iteration, beginning from 0, as a parameter. More importantly, the callback is fired in the context of the current DOM element, so the keyword `this` refers to that element.

Suppose we had a simple unordered list on the page:

```
<ul>
  <li>foo</li>
  <li>bar</li>
</ul>
```

We can select the list items and iterate across them:

```
$('li').each(function(index) {
  $(this).log(index + ': ' + $(this).text());
});
```

A message is thus logged for each item in the list:

```
0: foo
1: bar
```

The second syntax is similar, but it is a global function rather than a method. The collection is passed as the first parameter in this case, and can be either a map (JavaScript object) or an array. In the case of an array, the callback is passed an array index and corresponding array value as parameters each time:

```
$.each([52, 97], function(key, value) {
  $().log(key + ': ' + value);
});
```

This produces two messages:

```
0: 52
1: 97
```

If a map is used as the collection, the callback is passed a key-value pair as parameter each time:

```
$.each({'flammable': 'inflammable', 'duh': 'no duh'}, function(index,
value) {
  $().log(index + ': ' + value);
});
```

Once again, this produces two messages:

```
flammable: inflammable
duh: no duh
```

$.grep()

Winnow an array down to a selected set of items.

> `$.grep(array, filter[, invert])`

Parameters

- array: The array to search through
- filter: A function to apply as a test for each item, or a string containing an expression to use as a test
- invert (optional): A Boolean indicating whether to reverse the filter condition

Return Value

The newly constructed, filtered array.

Description

The `$.grep()` method removes items from an array as necessary so that all remaining items pass a provided test. The test is a function that is passed an array item and the index of the item within the array as parameters; only if the test returns true will the item be in the result array.

As is typical with jQuery methods, the callback function is often defined anonymously:

```
var array = [0, 1, 52, 97];
$(this).log('Before: ' + array);
array = $.grep(array, function(a) {
  return (a > 50);
});
$(this).log('After: ' + array);
```

All array items that are over 50 are preserved in the result array:

```
Before: 0,1,52,97
After: 52,97
```

Since filter functions tend to be very short, jQuery provides a further shortcut. Filter functions can be defined as a single expression that is evaluated for each item a in the array:

```
var array = [0, 1, 52, 97];
$(this).log('Before: ' + array);
array = $.grep(array, 'a > 50');
$(this).log('After: ' + array);
```

This produces the same results as before. We can invert this test by adding the third parameter:

```
var array = [0, 1, 52, 97];
$(this).log('Before: ' + array);
array = $.grep(array, 'a > 50', true);
$(this).log('After: ' + array);
```

This now produces an array of items less than or equal to 50:

```
Before: 0,1,52,97
After: 0,1
```

$.map()

Transform an array into another one by using a filter function.

```
$.map(array, filter)
```

Parameters
- array: The array to convert
- filter: A function to apply to each item, or a string containing an expression to apply

Return Value
The newly constructed, transformed array.

Description
The $.map() method applies a function to each item in an array, collecting the results into a new array. The filter is a function that is passed an array item and the index of the item within the array as parameters.

As is typical with jQuery methods, the callback function is often defined anonymously:

```
var array = [0, 1, 52, 97];
$(this).log('Before: ' + array);
array = $.map(array, function(a) {
  return (a - 45);
});
$(this).log('After: ' + array);
```

All array items are reduced by 45 in the result array:

```
Before: 0,1,52,97
After: -45,-44,7,52
```

Since filter functions tend to be very short, jQuery provides a further shortcut. Filter functions can be defined as a single expression that is applied to each item a in the array:

```
var array = [0, 1, 52, 97];
$(this).log('Before: ' + array);
array = $.map(array, 'a - 45');
$(this).log('After: ' + array);
```

This produces the same results as before. We can remove items from the array by returning null from the filter function:

```
var array = [0, 1, 52, 97];
$(this).log('Before: ' + array);
array = $.map(array, 'a > 50 ? a - 45 : null');
$(this).log('After: ' + array);
```

This now produces an array of the items that were greater than 50, each reduced by 45:

```
Before: 0,1,52,97
After: 7,52
```

If the filter function returns an array rather than a scalar, the returned arrays are concatenated together to form the result:

```
var array = [0, 1, 52, 97];
$(this).log('Before: ' + array);
array = $.map(array, function(a, i) {
  return [a - 45, i];
});
$(this).log('After: ' + array);
```

Instead of a two-dimensional result array, the map forms a flattened one:

```
Before: 0,1,52,97
After: -45,0,-44,1,7,2,52,3
```

$.merge()

> Merge the contents of two arrays together into the first array.
>
> ```
> $.merge(array1, array2)
> ```

Parameters

- array1: The first array to merge
- array2: The second array to merge

Return Value

An array consisting of elements from both supplied arrays.

Description

The $.merge() operation forms an array that contains all elements from the two arrays, with duplicates removed. The order of items in the first array is preserved, with items from the second array appended:

```
var array1 = [0, 1, 52];
var array2 = [52, 97];
$(this).log('Array 1: ' + array1);
$(this).log('Array 2: ' + array2);
array = $.merge(array1, array2);
$(this).log('After: ' + array);
```

The resulting array contains all four distinct items:

```
Array 1: 0,1,52
Array 2: 52,97
After: 0,1,52,97
```

The $.merge() function is destructive. It alters the first parameter to add the items from the second. If you need the original first array, make a copy of it before calling $.merge(). Fortunately, $.merge() itself can be used for this duplication:

```
var newArray = $.merge([], oldArray);
```

This shortcut creates a new, empty array and merges the contents of oldArray into it, effectively cloning the array.

$.unique()

Creates a copy of an array of objects with the duplicates removed.

    $.unique(array)

Parameters

- array: An array of objects

Return Value

An array consisting of only unique objects.

Description

The $.unique() function searches through an array of objects, forming a new array that does not contain duplicate objects. Two objects are considered distinct if they refer to different locations in memory, even if their contents are identical. The original array is not modified. The array may consist of any kind of JavaScript object:

```
var alice = {'alice': 'alice'};
var bob = {'bob': 'bob'};
var carol = {'carol': 'carol'};
var ted = {'bob': 'bob'};
var oldArray = [alice, bob, carol, bob, ted];
$(this).log('Before: ' + oldArray);
newArray = $.unique(oldArray);
$(this).log('After: ' + newArray);
```

The resulting array contains only the four distinct items:

```
Before: {alice: alice}, {bob: bob}, {carol: carol},
  {bob: bob}, {bob: bob}
After: {alice: alice, mergeNum: 52}, {bob: bob, mergeNum: 52},
  {carol: carol, mergeNum: 52}, {bob: bob, mergeNum: 52}
```

The second instance of the object named bob is removed from the resulting array. However, the object named ted remains even though it has identical content, since it was created as a separate object.

Note that $.unique() modifies the objects in the array, adding an extra property called mergeNum to each. This property is a side effect of the implementation of the function, and is not useful to the calling code.

$.extend()

Merge the contents of two objects together into the first object.

```
$.extend([target, ]properties[, ...])
```

Parameters

- target (optional): An object which will receive the new properties
- properties: An object containing additional properties to merge in

Return Value

The target object after it has been modified.

Description

The $.extend() function merges two objects in the same way that $.merge() merges arrays. The properties of the second object are added to the first, creating an object with all the properties of both objects:

```
var object1 = {
  apple: 0,
  banana: 52,
  cherry: 97
};
var object2 = {
  banana: 1,
  durian: 100
};

$().log(object1);
$().log(object2);
var object = $.extend(object1, object2);
$().log(object);
```

The value for durian in the second object gets added to the first, and the value for banana gets overwritten:

```
{apple: 0, banana: 52, cherry: 97, }
{banana: 1, durian: 100, }
{apple: 0, banana: 1, cherry: 97, durian: 100, }
```

The $.extend() function is destructive; the target object is modified in the process. This is generally desirable behavior, as $.extend() can in this way be used to simulate object inheritance. Methods added to the object become available to all the code that has a reference to the object. If, however, we want to preserve both of the original objects, we can do this by passing an empty object as the target:

```
var object = $.extend({}, object1, object2)
```

We can also supply more than two objects to `$.extend()`. In this case, properties from all of the objects are added to the target object.

If only one argument is supplied to `$.extend()`, this means the target argument was omitted. In this case, the jQuery object itself is assumed to be the target. By doing this, we can add new functions to the jQuery namespace. We will explore this capability when discussing how to create jQuery plug-ins.

The merge performed by `$.extend()` is not recursive; if a property of the first object is itself an object or an array, it will be completely overwritten by a property with the same key in the second object. The values are not merged.

$.trim()

Removes whitespace from the ends of a string.

```
$.trim()
```

Parameters

- string: A string to trim

Return Value

The trimmed string.

Description

The `$.trim()` function removes all newlines, spaces, and tabs from the beginning and end of the supplied string:

```
var string = "\tYes, no, I, this is. \n ";
$(this).log('Before: ' + string);
string = $.trim(string);
$(this).log('After: ' + string);
```

All of the whitespace characters are trimmed:

```
Before:    Yes, no, I, this is.

After: Yes, no, I, this is.
```

9
Plug-In API

I do two at a time now
I've developed a technique
                — Devo,
            "Fräulein"

Whenever a task is to be performed two or more times, it is a good idea to apply the
DRY principle—Don't Repeat Yourself. To facilitate this, jQuery provides several
tools for developers that go beyond simple iteration and function creation. **Plug-in**
development is a technique that proves rewarding time and time again.

In this chapter, we'll take a brief look at the basics of using another developer's
plug-in, and then delve into the various ways of extending jQuery with plug-ins we
define ourselves.

Using a Plug-in

Taking advantage of an existing jQuery plug-in is very straightforward. A plug-in
is contained in a standard JavaScript file. There are many ways to obtain the file,
but the simplest is to browse the jQuery plug-in repository at http://jquery.com/
plugins. The latest releases of many popular plug-ins are available for download
from this site.

To make a plug-in's methods available to us, we just include it in the <head> of the
document. We must ensure that it appears *after* the main jQuery source file, and
before our custom JavaScript code:

```
<head>
  <meta http-equiv="Content-Type" content="text/html;
                                            charset=utf-8"/>
  <script src="jquery.js" type="text/javascript"></script>
```

```
<script src="jquery.plug-in.js" type="text/javascript"></script>
<script src="custom.js" type="text/javascript"></script>
<title>Example</title>
</head>
```

After that, we're ready to use any of the methods made public by the plug-in. For example, using the *Form* plug-in, we can add a single line inside our custom file's $(document).ready method to submit a form via AJAX:

```
$(document).ready(function() {
  $('#myForm').ajaxForm();
});
```

Each plug-in is independently documented. In the subsequent chapters, we will examine a couple of the more prominent plug-ins in detail, describing each of their methods. To find out more about other plug-ins, we can explore the documentation linked from the jQuery plug-in repository, or read the explanatory comments found in the source code itself.

If we can't find the answers to all of our questions in the plug-in repository, the author's website, or the plug-in's comments, we can always turn to the jQuery discussion list. Many of the plug-in authors are frequent contributors to the list and are always willing to help with any problems that new users might face. Instructions for subscribing to the discussion list can be found at http://docs.jquery.com/Discussion.

Developing a Plug-in

As we discussed above, plug-in development is a useful technique whenever we are going to perform a task more than once. Here we will itemize the components that can populate a plug-in file of our own design. Our plug-ins can use any combination of the following four types of jQuery enhancements: object methods, global functions, selector expressions, and easing styles.

Object Method

Adds a new method to all jQuery objects created with the $() factory function.

```
jQuery.fn.methodName = methodDefinition;
```

Components

- `methodName`: A label for the new method.
- `methodDefinition`: A function object to execute when `.methodName()` is called on a jQuery object instance.

Discussion

When a function needs to act on one or more DOM elements, creating a new jQuery object method is usually appropriate. Object methods have access to the matched elements that are referenced by the jQuery object, and can inspect or manipulate them.

The jQuery object can be retrieved from within the method implementation by referencing the keyword `this`. We can either call the built-in jQuery methods of this object, or we can extract the DOM nodes to work with them directly. As we saw in Chapter 8, we can retrieve a referenced DOM node using array notation:

```
jQuery.fn.showAlert = function() {
  alert('You called the method on "' + this[0] + '".');
  return this;
}
```

Here, we use `this[0]` to find one element, but we need to remember that a jQuery selector expression can always match zero, one, or multiple elements. We must allow room for any of these scenarios when designing a plug-in method. The easiest way to accomplish this is to call `.each()` on the method context; this enforces **implicit iteration**, which is important for maintaining consistency between plug-in and built-in methods. Within the function argument of the `.each()` call, `this` refers to each DOM element in turn:

```
jQuery.fn.showAlert = function() {
  return this.each(function() {
    alert('You called the method on "' + this + '".');
  });
}
```

Now we can apply our method to a jQuery object referencing multiple items:

```
$('.myClass').showAlert();
```

Our method produces a separate alert for each element that was matched by the preceding selector expression.

Note also that in these examples, we return the jQuery object itself (referenced by `this`) when we are done with our work. This enables the **chaining** behavior that jQuery users should be able to rely on. We must return a jQuery object from all plug-in methods, unless the method is clearly intended to retrieve a different piece of information and is documented as such.

Global Function

Makes a new function available to scripts, contained within the jQuery namespace.

```
jQuery.pluginName = fnDefinition;

jQuery.pluginName = {

  function1: fnDefinition1,

  function2: fnDefinition2

};
```

Components (First Version)

- `pluginName`: The name of the current plug-in.
- `fnDefinition`: A function object to execute when `$.pluginName()` is called.

Components (Second Version)

- `pluginName`: The name of the current plug-in.
- `function1`: A label for the first function.
- `fnDefinition1`: A function object to execute when `$.pluginName.function1()` is called.
- `function2`: A label for the second function.
- `fnDefinition2`: A function object to execute when `$.pluginName.function2()` is called.

Discussion

What we call **global functions** here are technically methods of the `jQuery` function object. Practically speaking, they are functions within a jQuery namespace. By placing the function within the jQuery namespace, we reduce the chance of name conflicts with other functions and variables in scripts.

Single Functions

The first usage opposite illustrates the creation of a global function when the plug-in needs only a single function. By using the plug-in name as the function name, we can ensure that our function definition will not be trod on by other plug-ins (as long as the others follow the same guideline!). The new function is assigned as a property of the jQuery function object:

```
jQuery.myPlugin = function() {
  alert('This is a test. This is only a test.');
};
```

Now in any code that uses this plug-in, we can write:

```
jQuery.myPlugin();
```

We can also use the $ alias and write:

```
$.myPlugin();
```

This will work just like any other function call, and the alert will be displayed.

Multiple Functions

In the second usage, we see how to define global functions when more than one is needed by the same plug-in. We encapsulate all of the plug-ins within a single namespace, named after our plug-in:

```
jQuery.myPlugin = {
  foo: function() {
    alert('This is a test. This is only a test.');
  },
  bar: function(param) {
    alert('This function takes a parameter, which is "'
                                        + param + '".');
  }
};
```

To invoke these functions, we address them as members of an object named after our plug-in, which is itself a property of the global jQuery function object:

```
$.myPlugin.foo();
$.myPlugin.bar('baz');
```

Functions are now properly protected from collisions with other functions and variables in the global namespace.

In general, it is wise to use this second usage from the start, even if it seems that only one function will be needed, as it makes future expansion easier.

Selector Expression

Adds a new way to find DOM elements using a jQuery selector string.

```
jQuery.extend(jQuery.expr[selectorType], {
    selectorName: elementTest
});
```

Components

- `selectorType`: The prefix character for the selector string, which indicates which type of selector is being defined. In practice, the useful value for plug-ins is `':'`, which indicates a pseudo-class selector.
- `selectorName`: A string uniquely identifying this selector.
- `elementTest`: A string containing a JavaScript expression to evaluate. If the expression evaluates to `true` for an element `a`, that element will be included in the resulting set; otherwise, the element will be excluded.

Discussion

Plug-ins can add selector expressions that allow scripts to find specific sets of DOM elements using a compact syntax. Generally, the expressions that plug-ins add are new pseudo-classes, identified by a leading `':'` character.

The pseudo-classes that are supported by jQuery have the general format `:selectorName(param1(param2))`. Only the `selectorName` portion of this format is required; `param1` and `param2` are available if the pseudo-class allows parameters to make it more specific.

The element test expression can refer to two special variables, named `a` and `m`. The DOM element being tested is stored in `a`, and the components of the selector expression are held in `m`. The contents of `m` are the result of a regular expression match, which breaks `:selectorName(param1(param2))` down as follows:

```
m[0]  ==  ':selectorName(param1(param2))'
m[1]  ==  ':'
m[2]  ==  'selectorName'
m[3]  ==  'param1(param2)'
m[4]  ==  '(param2)'
```

For example, we can build a pseudo-class that tests the number of child nodes of an element, and call this new selector expression `:num-children(n)`:

```
jQuery.extend(jQuery.expr[':'], {
    'num-children': 'a.childNodes.length == m[3]'
});
```

Now we can, for example, select all `<ul>` elements with exactly two child nodes, and turn them red:

```
$(document).ready(function() {
  $('ul:num-children(2)').css('color', 'red');
});
```

If it is necessary to add selector expressions other than pseudo-classes, `jQuery.parse` inside `jquery.js` should be consulted to find the relevant regular expression matches for other selector types.

Easing Style

Defines an acceleration curve for future animations.

```
jQuery.extend(jQuery.easing, {

  easingStyleName: easingFunction

});
```

Components

- `easingStyleName`: A label for the new easing style.
- `easingFunction`: A function object that determines the animation value at any given moment. Easing functions are passed the following arguments:
  - `fraction`: The current position of the animation, as measured in time between 0 (the beginning of the animation) and 1 (the end of the animation).
  - `elapsed`: The number of milliseconds that have passed since the beginning of the animation (seldom used).
  - `attrStart`: The beginning value of the CSS attribute that is being animated.
  - `attrDelta`: The difference between the start and end values of the CSS attribute that is being animated.
  - `duration`: The total number of milliseconds that will pass during the animation (seldom used).

Discussion

Most effect methods trigger an animation with a fixed **easing style**, called **swing**. An easing style defines how the animation will speed up and slow down over time. The `.animate` method gives us more flexibility; a parameter to the method allows a custom easing style to be specified. New easing styles can be created using this plug-in mechanism.

An easing function must return the value of the property being animated at any moment within the animation. Because of the arguments that are passed to an easing function, the calculation usually takes the form:

```
f(fraction) * attrDelta + attrStart
```

In this calculation, `f` represents a mathematical function whose value varies from 0 to 1 as its parameter varies from 0 to 1. For example, an easing style that caused the animation to proceed at a constant rate would require a linear function (`f(x) = x`):

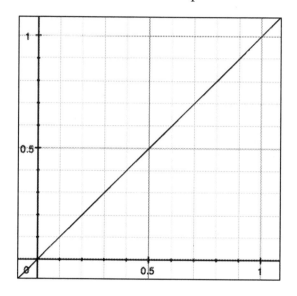

In a plug-in, this easing style would be expressed with the following code:

```
jQuery.extend(jQuery.easing, {
    'linear': function(fraction, elapsed, attrStart, attrDelta,
                                                        duration) {
        return fraction * attrDelta + attrStart;
    }
});
```

On the other hand, if we wished our animation to begin slowly and speed up gradually, we could use a quadratic function ($f(x) = x^2$):

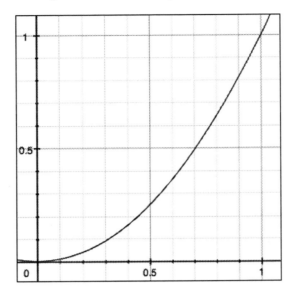

In a plug-in, this easing style would be expressed with the following code:

```
jQuery.extend(jQuery.easing, {
    'quadratic': function(fraction, elapsed, attrStart, attrDelta,
                                                        duration) {
      return fraction * fraction * attrDelta + attrStart;
    }
});
```

With an easing plug-in such as this one installed, we can choose the new easing style any time we invoke the .animate method:

```
$('.myClass').animate({
    'left': 500,
    'opacity': 0.1
}, 'slow', 'quadratic');
```

With this call, all elements with a class of myClass attached will move and fade to the specified values, starting slowly and speeding up gradually until they reach their destinations.

Example: Maintaining Multiple Event Logs

In the various examples in preceding reference chapters, we have had the need to display log events when various events occur. JavaScript's `alert` function is often used for this type of demonstration, but does not allow for the frequent, timely messages we needed on occasion. A better alternative is the `console.log` function available to Firefox and Safari, which allows printing messages to a separate log that does not interrupt the flow of interaction on the page. As this function is not available to Internet Explorer, however, we used a custom function to achieve this style of message logging.

> The Firebug Lite script (described in Appendix B) provides a very robust cross-platform logging facility. The method we develop here is tailored specifically for the examples in the preceding chapters; for general utility, Firebug Lite is typically preferable.

A simple way to log messages would be to create a global function that appends messages to a specific element on the page:

```
jQuery.log = function(message) {
  $('<div class="log-message"></div>')
    .text(message).appendTo('.log');
};
```

We can get a bit fancier, and have the new message appear with an animation:

```
jQuery.log = function(message) {
  $('<div class="log-message"></div>')
    .text(message)
    .hide()
    .appendTo('.log')
    .fadeIn();
};
```

Now we can call `$.log('foo')` to display `foo` in the log box on the page.

We sometimes had multiple examples on a single page, however, and it was convenient to be able to keep separate logs for each example. We accomplished this by using a method rather than global function:

```
jQuery.fn.log = function(message) {
  return this.each(function() {
    $('<div class="log-message"></div>')
```

```
        .text(message)
        .hide()
        .appendTo(this)
        .fadeIn();
    });
};
```

Now calling $('.log').log('foo') has the effect our global function call did previously, but we can change the selector expression to target different log boxes.

Ideally, though, the .log method would be intelligent enough to locate the most relevant box to use for the log message without an explicit selector. By exploiting the context passed to the method, we can traverse the DOM to find the log box nearest the selected element:

```
jQuery.fn.log = function(message) {
    return this.each(function() {
        $context = $(this);
        while ($context.length) {
            $log = $context.find('.log');
            if ($log.length) {
                $('<div class="log-message"></div>')
                    .text(message).hide().appendTo($log).fadeIn();
                break;
            }
            $context = $context.parent();
        }
    });
};
```

This code looks for a log message box within the matched elements, and if none is found, walks up the DOM in search of one.

Finally, at times we require the ability to display the contents of an object. Printing out the object itself yields something barely informative like [object Object], so we can detect the argument type and do some of our own pretty-printing in the case that an object is passed in:

```
jQuery.fn.log = function(message) {
    if (typeof(message) == 'object') {
        string = '{';
        $.each(message, function(key, value) {
            string += key + ': ' + value + ', ';
        });
        string += '}';
        message = string;
```

```
    }
    return this.each(function() {
      $context = $(this);
      while ($context.length) {
        $log = $context.find('.log');
        if ($log.length) {
          $('<div class="log-message"></div>')
            .text(message).hide().appendTo($log).fadeIn();
          break;
        }
        $context = $context.parent();
      }
    });
  };
```

Now we have a method that can be used to write out both objects and strings in a place that is relevant to the work being done on the page.

Summary

We've viewed plug-ins from two angles in this chapter: usage and development. We've looked at four types of additions we can make to jQuery with our own plug-ins. Plug-ins can introduce new global methods and jQuery object methods; moreover, they can add selector expressions and easing styles.

Often, though, we'll be more interested in using plug-ins that others have created. While we've already pointed to available documentation for many plug-ins, we will go into more detail about two of the more popular ones in the following chapters.

10

Dimensions Plug-In

The symbols we believe in
Sometimes turn inside out
Reshaping each dimension
We're so sure about
                    — Devo,
          "Plain Truth"

The **Dimensions** plug-in, co-authored by Paul Bakaus and Brandon Aaron, helps bridge the gap between the CSS box model and developers' need to accurately measure the height and the width of elements in a document. It also measures with pixel accuracy the top and left offsets of elements, no matter where they are found on the page. In this chapter, we'll explore this plug-in's various methods and discuss their options.

Size Methods

In addition to determining the dimensions of the browser window or the document, the following size methods form a powerful set of tools for identifying an element's height and width, whether we want to take into account the element's padding and border sizes or not.

We'll be using the same basic HTML for each of the examples that follow:

```
<body>
  <div id="container">
<!-- CODE CONTINUES -->
    <div id="content">
      <div class="dim-outer">
        <p>This is the outer dimensions box. It has the following CSS
                                                          rule:</p>
```

```
<pre><code>.dim-outer {
  height: 200px;
  width: 200px;
  margin: 10px;
  padding: 1em;
  border: 5px solid #e3e3e3;
  overflow: auto;
  font-size: 12px;
}</code></pre>
        <p>Scroll down for the inner dimensions box.</p>
        <p>Lorem ipsum dolor sit amet, consectetur adipisicing elit,
           sed do eiusmod tempor incididunt ut labore et dolore magna
           aliqua. Ut enim ad minim veniam, quis nostrud exercitation
           ullamco laboris nisi ut aliquip ex ea commodo consequat.
           Duis aute irure dolor in reprehenderit in voluptate velit
           esse cillum dolore eu fugiat nulla pariatur. Excepteur
           sint occaecat cupidatat non proident, sunt in culpa qui
           officia deserunt mollit anim id est laborum.</p>
        <div class="dim-inner"> This is the inner dimensions box.
        </div>
      </div>

<!-- CODE CONTINUES -->

    </div>
  </div>
</body>
```

.height()

Gets the height of the `document` or `window` object.

`.height()`

Parameters

None.

Return Value

An integer representing the height in pixels.

Discussion

The `.height` method simply uses the jQuery core method of the same name when applied to elements. Dimensions extends the use of `.height()` to the browser `window` and the `document` as well.

`$(window).height()` returns the pixel height of the browser window. If there is a horizontal scrollbar, it is not included in the height calculation.

`$(document).height()` returns the pixel height of the document. If the document has a greater height than the viewable area—in which case a vertical scrollbar is present—`$(document).height()` calculates the total height, including both the visible and the hidden parts.

The following image illustrates the difference between `$(document).height()` and `$(window).height()`:

For information on using the `.height` method with elements on the page, see Chapter 4.

.width()

Gets the width of the document or window object.

```
.width()
```

Parameters

None.

Return Value

An integer representing the width in pixels.

Description

The `.width` method, like its `.height()` counterpart, simply uses the jQuery core method of the same name when it is applied to elements. However, Dimensions extends `.width()` so that we can apply it to the `document` and the browser `window`, as well.

`$(document).width()` returns the pixel width of the document alone. If there is a vertical scrollbar, `$(document).width()` does not include it in the calculation. If the document has a greater width than the viewable area—in which case a horizontal scrollbar is present—`$(document).width()` calcuflates the total height, including both the visible and the hidden part of the page.

`$(window).width()` returns the pixel width of the browser. If there is a vertical scrollbar, it is not included in the width calculation.

The following image illustrates the difference between `$(document).width()` and `$(window).width()`:

For information on using the `.width` method with elements on the page, see Chapter 4.

.innerHeight()

> Gets the computed inner height for the first element in the set of matched elements.
>
> `.innerHeight()`

Parameters

None.

Return Value

An integer representing the inner height of the element, in pixels.

Description

The `.innerHeight` method differs from the basic `.height()` in that it calculates the height of the top and bottom padding in addition to the element itself. It does not, however, include the border or margin in the calculation.

If used with `document` or `window`, `.innerHeight()` calls the Dimensions `.height` method to return the value.

Given an element with a height of `200px`, font size of `12px`, and top and bottom padding of `1em`, `.innerHeight()` returns `224` (pixels), as can be seen in the following illustration:

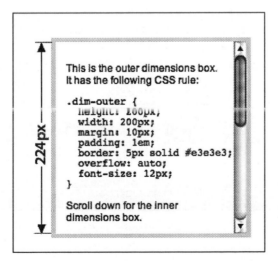

.innerWidth()

Gets the computed inner width for the first element in the set of matched elements.

    .innerWidth()

Parameters

None.

Return Value

An integer representing the inner width of the element, in pixels.

Description

The .innerWidth method differs from the basic .width() in that it calculates the width of the left and right padding in addition to the element itself. It does not, however, include the border or margin in the calculation.

If used with document or window, .innerWidth() calls the Dimensions .width method to return the value.

Given an element with a width of 200px, font size of 12px, and left and right padding of 1em, .innerWidth() returns 224 (pixels), as can be seen in the following illustration:

.outerHeight()

Gets the computed outer height of the first element in the set of matched elements.

```
.outerHeight()
```

Parameters

None.

Return Value

An integer representing the outer height of the element, in pixels.

Discussion

The `.outerHeight` method differs from the basic `.height()` in that it calculates the height of the top and bottom padding and the top and bottom borders in addition to the element itself. Like `.height()` and `.innerHeight()`, however, it does not include the element's margins in the calculation.

If used with `document` or `window`, `.outerHeight()` calls the Dimensions `.height` method to return the value.

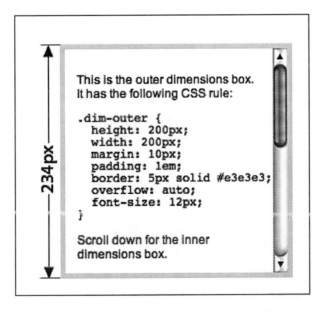

.outerWidth()

Gets the computed outer width for the first element in the set of
matched elements.

    .outerWidth()

Parameters

None.

Return Value

An integer representing the outer width of the element, in pixels.

Description

The .outerWidth method differs from the basic .width() in that it calculates the
width of the left and right padding and the left and right borders in addition to the
element itself. Like .width() and .innerWidth(), however, it does not include the
element's margins in the calculations.

If used with document or window, .outerWidth() calls the Dimensions .width
method to return the value.

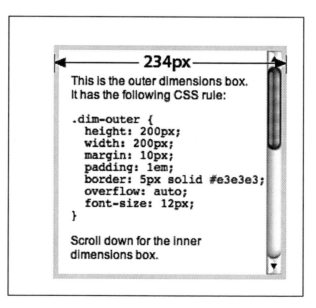

Position Methods

The following methods are helpful in determining the exact positioning of elements—in relation to a positioned ancestor, the document body, or the viewable area of the document.

As in the *Size Methods* section, we'll be using the same basic HTML for each of the following examples:

```
<body>
  <div id="container">
<!-- CODE CONTINUES -->
    <div id="content">
      <div class="dim-outer">
        <p>This is the outer dimensions box. It has the
                                      following CSS rule:</p>
<pre><code>.dim-outer {
  height: 200px;
  width: 200px;
  margin: 10px;
  padding: 1em;
  border: 5px solid #e3e3e3;
  overflow: auto;
  font-size: 12px;
}</code></pre>
        <p>Scroll down for the inner dimensions box.</p>
        <p>Lorem ipsum dolor sit amet, consectetur adipisicing elit,
           sed do eiusmod tempor incididunt ut labore et dolore magna
           aliqua. Ut enim ad minim veniam, quis nostrud exercitation
           ullamco laboris nisi ut aliquip ex ea commodo consequat.
           Duis aute irure dolor in reprehenderit in voluptate velit
           esse cillum dolore eu fugiat nulla pariatur. Excepteur
           sint occaecat cupidatat non proident, sunt in culpa qui
           officia deserunt mollit anim id est laborum.</p>
        <div class="dim-inner"> This is the inner dimensions box.
        </div>
      </div>

<!-- CODE CONTINUES -->

    </div>
  </div>
</body>
```

.scrollTop()

Gets the number of pixels that the window or a scrollable element within the document has been scrolled down.

`.scrollTop()`

Parameters

None.

Return Value

An integer representing the vertical scrollbar position in pixels.

Discussion

The `.scrollTop` method is able to return the vertical scroll position of either the browser window or an element within the document. For example, given `<div class="dim-outer">` after it has been scrolled down 96 pixels (as shown in the following image), `$('div.dim-outer').scrollTop()` returns 96:

```
    margin: 10px;
    padding: 1em;
    border: 5px solid #e3e3e3;
    overflow: auto;
    font-size: 12px;
}

Scroll down for the inner
dimensions box.

Lorem ipsum dolor sit amet,
consectetur adipisicing elit, sed
do eiusmod tempor incididunt ut
labore et dolore magna aliqua. Ut
enim ad minim veniam, quis
nostrud exercitation ullamco
laboris nisi ut aliquip ex ea
```

.scrollTop(value)

Sets the number of pixels to be scrolled down in the window or or the matched set of scrollable element within a document.

`.scrollTop(value)`

Parameters

- `value`: An integer representing the number of pixels.

Return Value

The jQuery object, for chaining purposes.

Description

By passing in a numeric value to the `.scrollTop` method, we can move the scroll position of the browser window or scrollable elements within the document up or down. In the following image, the scroll position of `<div class="dim-outer">` has been set with `$('div.dim-outer').scrollTop(200)`:

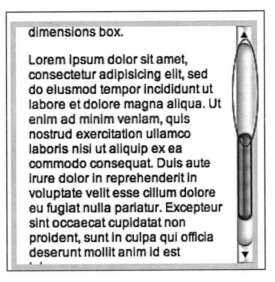

.scrollLeft()

> Gets the number of pixels that the window or a scrollable element within the document has been scrolled from left to right.
>
> `.scrollLeft()`

Parameters

None.

Return Value

An integer representing the horizontal scrollbar position in pixels.

Description

The .scrollLeft method is able to return the horizontal scroll position of either the browser window or an element within the document. For example, after the browser window has been scrolled to the right 24 pixels, as shown in the following image, the return value of $(window).scrollLeft() is 24:

.scrollLeft(value)

Sets the number of pixels to be scrolled from left to right in the window or the matched set of scrollable elements within a document.

```
.scrollLeft(value)
```

Parameters

* value: An integer representing the number of pixels.

Return Value

The jQuery object, for chaining purposes.

Discussion

By passing in a numeric value to the .scrollLeft method, we can move the scroll position of the browser window or scrollable elements within the document left or right. In the following image, the scroll position of the browser window has been set with $(window).scrollLeft(50)

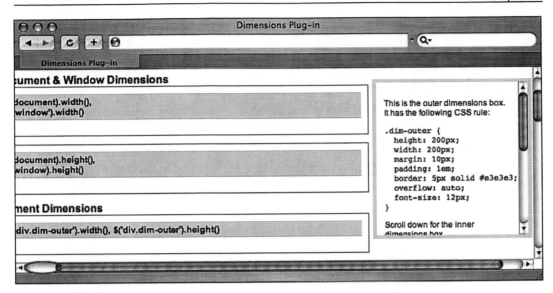

.offset()

Gets the top and left coordinates of the first element in the set of matched elements. Also gets the matched element's `scrollTop` and `scrollLeft` offsets.

```
.offset([options])
```

```
.offset(options, returnObject)
```

Parameters (First Version)

- `options` (optional): A map of settings to configure the way the offset is calculated. Can contain the following items:

  - `margin` (optional): A Boolean indicating whether to include the element's margin in the calculations. Default is `true`.

  - `border` (optional): A Boolean indicating whether to include the element's border in the calculations. Default is `false`.

  - `padding` (optional): A Boolean indicating whether to include the element's padding in the calculations. Default is `false`.

  - `scroll` (optional): A Boolean indicating whether to include the scroll offsets of all ancestor elements in the calculations. Default is `true`.

  - `lite` (optional): A Boolean indicating whether to use offsetLite instead of offset. Default is `false`.

- `relativeTo` (optional): An HTML element representing the ancestor element relative to which the matched element will be offset. Default is `document.body`.

Parameters (Second Version)

- `options`: A map of settings to configure the way the offset is calculated.
    - `margin` (optional): A Boolean indicating whether to include the element's margin in the calculations. Default is `true`.
    - `border` (optional): A Boolean indicating whether to include the element's border in the calculations. Default is `false`.
    - `padding` (optional): A Boolean indicating whether to include the element's padding in the calculations. Default is `false`.
    - `scroll` (optional): A Boolean indicating whether to include the scroll offsets of all ancestor elements in the calculations. Default is `true`.
    - `lite` (optional): A Boolean indicating whether to use `offsetLite` instead of `offset`. Default is `false`.
    - `relativeTo` (optional): An HTML element representing the ancestor element relative to which the matched element will be offset. Default is `document.body`.
    - `returnObject`: An object in which to store the return value. When the second version of the method is used, the chain will not be broken, and the result will be assigned to this object.

Return Value (First Version)

An object containing values for `top`, `left`, and optionally `scrollTop` and `scrollLeft`.

Return Value (Second Version)

The jQuery object, for chaining purposes.

Description

The `.offset` method allows us to locate the `top` and `left` positions of any element anywhere on the page, whether its `position` is `static` or `relative`, `absolute` or `fixed`, and regardless of the position of scrollbars. With options for factoring margin, border, padding, and scroll into the calculation, `.offset()` provides great flexibility as well as accuracy.

The following series of images demonstrates the different values returned by `.offset()` depending on how the options are set.

Defaults

In the first example, the default settings for padding (`false`), border (`false`), and margin (`true`) are used. The result:

```
{top: 117, left: 580, scrollTop: 0, scrollLeft: 0}
```

Note here that since the default for margin is `true`, the distance from the left edge of the window to the matched element extends all the way to (but not including) the element's border.

Including Border

In the second example, the border option is set to `true`. Since `<div class="dim-outer">` has a 5-pixel border around it, the `top` and `left` values increase by 5 pixels each:

```
{top: 122, left: 585, scrollTop: 0, scrollLeft: 0}
```

Including Border and Padding

The next example sets both the border and padding options to `true` (remember that the margin option's value is `true` by default). The result is an increase, again, of 5 pixels for the borders and another 12 pixels (`1em`) for the padding:

```
{top: 134, left: 597, scrollTop: 0, scrollLeft: 0}
```

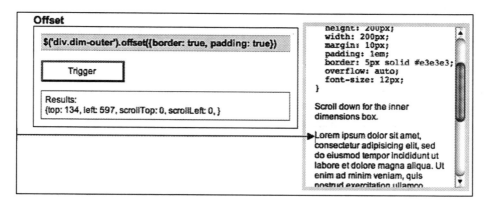

Finding the Position Relative to an Ancestor

With the `relativeTo` option, we can find the offset distance between an element and any one of its positioned ancestors. In the next example, we're getting the offset between `<div class="dim-outer">` and `<div id="content">`. Since this `content` `<div>` is itself offset from the left side of the window due to a container's 24-pixel left margin, the value of `left` is now 24 pixels less than that of the previous example:

```
{top: 27, left: 573, scrollTop: 0, scrollLeft: 0}
```

Offset

```
var theContent = $('#content')[0];
$('div.dim-outer').offset({border: true, padding: true, relativeTo: theContent})
```

Trigger

Results:
{top: 27, left: 573, scrollTop: 0, scrollLeft: 0, }

```
height: 200px;
width: 200px;
margin: 10px;
padding: 1em;
border: 5px solid #e3e3e3;
overflow: auto;
font-size: 12px;
}
```

Scroll down for the inner dimensions box.

Lorem ipsum dolor sit amet, consectetur adipisicing elit, sed do eiusmod tempor incididunt ut labore et dolore magna aliqua. Ut enim ad minim veniam, quis nostrud exercitation ullamco

It's worth noting here that, since the `relativeTo` setting takes a DOM element, we used the shorthand `[0]` notation to convert a jQuery object to a DOM element before using it for the `relativeTo` argument.

The `top` value of 27 is derived from the sum of the floated `<div class="dim-outer">` element's margin (12), border (5), and padding (10). If `<div id="content">` had any top padding applied to it, that would be added to the total top offset as well.

Returning Scroll Offsets

The `scroll` option, which has a default value of `true`, is particularly useful when the matched element is inside one or more elements that have the `overflow` property set to `auto` or `scroll`. It adds the total scroll offsets of all ancestor elements to the total offset and adds two properties to the returned object, `scrollTop` and `scrollLeft`. Its usefulness can be observed in the following example showing the offset of `<div class="dim-inner">` when `<div class="dim-outer">` has been scrolled down 79 pixels:

```
{top: 509, left: 597, scrollTop: 79, scrollLeft: 0}
```

Maintaining Chainability

If we wish to pass in a return object in order to continue chaining methods, we must still include the options map. To keep the default values intact for those options while passing in a return object, we can simply use an empty map. For example, `$('div.dim-outer').offset({}, returnObject)` obtains the same values as `$('div.dim-outer').offset()`, but stores them in `returnObject` for later use.

Suppose we want to get the offset and scroll values of `<div class="dim-outer">` while changing its background color to gray (`#cccccc`) at the same time. The code would look like this:

```
var retObj = {};
$('div.dim-outer')
  .offset({}, retObj)
  .css('background','#ccc');
$(this).log(retObj);
```

We start by declaring a variable for the return object (retObj). Then we chain the .offset and .css methods to the selector. Finally, we do something with the object returned by .offset() — in this case, log the results with our Log plug-in. The <div>'s background color is changed and the .offset() values are logged as follows:

{top: 117, left: 580, scrollTop: 0, scrollLeft: 0}

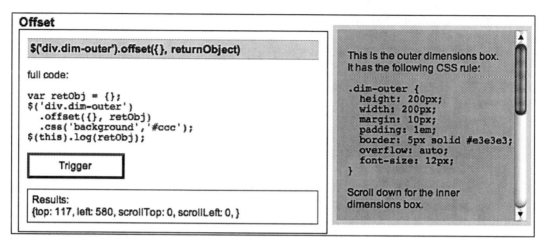

.position()

> Gets the position of the first element in the matched set of elements, relative to its nearest relative-, absolute- or fixed-positioned ancestor.
>
> .position()
>
> .position(returnObject)

Parameters (First Version)

None.

Parameters (Second Version)

- returnObject: An object in which to store the return value. When the second version of the method is used, the chain will not be broken, and the result will be assigned to this object.

Return Value (First Version)

An object containing values for top and left.

Return Value (Second Version)

The jQuery object, for chaining purposes.

Description

The `.position` method is shorthand for the following `.offset()` variation:

```
.offset({
  margin: false,
  scroll: false,
  relativeTo: offsetParent
  },
  returnObject);
```

Here, only the element's top and left position—without any padding, border, or margin—is determined in relation to its nearest positioned ancestor. For more details on these options, see the description of `.offset()`.

For `relativeTo`, the `.position()` method uses a variable, `offsetParent`, which is set in the Dimensions code. Effectively, this code begins with the element's immediate parent and crawls up the DOM, stopping at the first element that has a position of `relative`, `absolute`, or `fixed`. The initial element's offset position is then calculated in relation to that nearest positioned element.

Consider the following HTML:

```
<div id="outer">
  <div id="middle" style="position: relative">
    <div id="inner">
      <p>Use .position() for this paragraph</p>
    </div>
  </div>
</div>
```

Using `$('p').position()` calculates the top and left offsets of the paragraph in relation to `<div id="middle">` because that `<div>` is the nearest positioned ancestor (note its `style` attribute).

Since `.position()` takes no parameters (except `returnValue` in the second version), it is much less flexible than `.offset()`. In most cases, `.offset()`, which was discussed above, is recommended.

11
Form Plug-In

You better find out
Before you fill in the blanks
                — Devo,
        "Find Out"

The **Form** plug-in is a terrific example of a script that makes a difficult, complex task dead simple. It assists us in AJAX submission of forms (even if the forms contain file upload fields), as well as inspection and manipulation of the contents of form fields.

AJAX Form Submission

These methods assist in submitting a form's contents to the server using AJAX calls.

.ajaxSubmit()

Sends a form's contents to the server without a page refresh.
```
.ajaxSubmit(success)
.ajaxSubmit(options)
```

Parameters (First Version)

- `success`: A callback to execute when the server successfully responds.

Parameters (Second Version)

- `options`: A map of options configuring the submission. Can contain the following items:
    - `url` (optional): The URL to which the form will be submitted. The default value is the form's `action` attribute value, or the current page's URL if none is found.

- ○ type (optional): The method to use when submitting the form (GET or POST). The default value is the form's method attribute value, or GET if none is found.

- ○ beforeSubmit (optional): A callback to execute before the request is sent.

- ○ dataType (optional): How the response data will be interpreted. Can be 'xml', 'script', or 'json'.

- ○ target (optional): The element into which the response HTML will be placed. Can be a selector string, jQuery object, or DOM element reference. Only valid if dataType is omitted.

- ○ success (optional): A callback to execute when the server successfully responds.

- ○ semantic (optional): Whether to force strict HTML ordering of fields. The default value is false.

- ○ resetForm (optional): A Boolean indicating whether to reset the form values to their defaults after a successful submission. The default value is false.

- ○ clearForm (optional): A Boolean indicating whether to clear the form values after a successful submission. The default value is false.

Return Value

The jQuery object, for chaining purposes.

Discussion

The .ajaxSubmit method issues an AJAX request using the provided url and type information, along with the data currently present in the form. The form contents are encoded using the .formToArray method, and intricacies such as file uploading are handled behind the scenes.

If a callback is provided using the beforeSubmit option, the callback will be fired before the request is sent. This gives us an opportunity to perform last-minute validation or cleanup. If a validation routine detects errors that the user must correct, the routine can return false to prevent the form from being submitted. The callback is passed the form data as returned by .formToArray(), the jQuery object that references the form, and the options object that was provided to .ajaxSubmit(). For an example of this callback in action, see the example in the discussion of .ajaxForm() later.

When a `dataType` is provided, the response data is interpreted accordingly. The processing performed is the same as with the `$.ajax` function for the supported data types. Any `script` responses are interpreted as JavaScript and executed in the global context, while `json` responses are parsed as a JavaScript object or array. Calls that specify an `xml` data type do not cause any parsing to occur when the response is received.

If no `dataType` is provided, then we can instead use the `target` option. The DOM element referred to by the target will be filled with the response to the AJAX request, interpreted as plain HTML. The `dataType` and `target` options are mutually exclusive.

After any relevant processing has been performed due to the `dataType` or `target` options, the `success` callback is executed. This function is given the response data to act on. For information on ways to interpret and manipulate the response data, see the `$.ajax` function discussion in Chapter 7.

The `semantic` flag forces strict semantic ordering at the expense of execution speed. For more information, see the `.formToArray()` discussion later.

If `resetForm` or `clearForm` is set to `true`, the corresponding action will be taken before the `success` callback (if provided) is executed. For more information on these actions, see the `.clearForm` and `.resetForm` method discussions later.

If the form that is being submitted contains file upload fields, the file data will be properly uploaded using the `multipart/form-data` MIME type. No further action needs to be taken.

Note that the `.ajaxSubmit` method executes immediately. Since it is common to issue the AJAX request when the submit button is clicked, it is typically more convenient to use the `.ajaxForm` method instead. However, the direct action of `.ajaxSubmit()` may be the easiest way to achieve interaction between this plug-in and others, such as the popular **Validation** plug-in.

.ajaxForm()

Prepares a form for automatic AJAX submission.

```
.ajaxForm(options)
```

Parameters

- `options`: A map of options configuring the submission. Can contain the following items (which are passed along intact to `.ajaxSubmit()`):
  - ○ `url` (optional): The URL to which the form will be submitted. The default value is the form's `action` attribute value, or the current page's URL if none is found.
  - ○ `type` (optional): The method to use when submitting the form (GET or POST). The default value is the form's `method` attribute value, or GET if none is found.
  - ○ `beforeSubmit` (optional): A callback to execute before the request is sent.
  - ○ `dataType` (optional): How the response data will be interpreted. Can be `'xml'`, `'script'`, or `'json'`.
  - ○ `target` (optional): The element into which the response HTML will be placed. Can be a selector string, jQuery object, or DOM element reference. Only valid if `dataType` is omitted.
  - ○ `success` (optional): A callback to execute when the server successfully responds.
  - ○ `semantic` (optional): Whether to force strict HTML ordering of fields. The default value is `false`.
  - ○ `resetForm` (optional): A Boolean indicating whether to reset the form values to their defaults after a successful submission. The default value is `false`.
  - ○ `clearForm` (optional): A Boolean indicating whether to clear the form values after a successful submission. The default value is `false`.

Return Value

The jQuery object, for chaining purposes.

Discussion

The `.ajaxForm` method prepares a form for later submission by AJAX. When the form is submitted, the AJAX request will use the provided `url` and `type` information, along with the data currently present in the form. The form contents are encoded using the `.formToArray` method, and intricacies such as file uploading are handled behind the scenes.

Unlike the .ajaxSubmit method, the .ajaxForm method does not cause immediate action. Instead, it binds handlers to the submit event of the form and the click events of form buttons, which in turn cause the form contents to be sent as an AJAX request. This removes some of the work in setting up an AJAX form.

In addition, the .ajaxForm method is able to simulate other aspects of a standard form submission that the .ajaxSubmit method cannot. The name and value of the submit button that was clicked are included with the request when .ajaxForm() does the job. Also, when a form contains an <input> field of type image, .ajaxForm() can capture the mouse coordinates and send them along with the request.

For best results, the **Dimensions** plug-in should also be present when using image inputs. The Form plug-in will auto-detect the presence of Dimensions and use it if possible.

The .ajaxForm method can be used with forms containing any standard field type:

```
<form id="test-form" name="test-form" action="submit.php"
                                                method="post">
  <div class="form-row">
    <label for="city">City</label>
    <input type="text" id="city" name="city" size="20" />
  </div>
  <div class="form-row">
    <label for="state">State</label>
    <input type="text" id="state" name="state" size="5" value="MI" />
  </div>
  <div class="form-row">
    <label for="comment">Comments</label>
    <textarea id="comment" name="comment" rows="8" cols="30">
    </textarea>
  </div>

  <div class="form-row">
    <label for="sacks">Villages sacked</label>
    <select name="villages" id="villages">
      <option value="0">none</option>
      <option value="5" selected="selected">1-5</option>
      <option value="10">6-10</option>
      <option value="20">11-20</option>
      <option value="50">21-50</option>
      <option value="100">51-100</option>
      <option value="more">over 100</option>
    </select>
  </div>
```

```
<div class="form-row multi">
  <span class="multi-label">Preferred tactic</span>
  <input type="radio" name="tactic" value="loot" id="loot"
            checked="checked" /><label for="loot">loot</label>
  <input type="radio" name="tactic" value="pillage" id="pillage" />
                          <label for="pillage">pillage</label>
  <input type="radio" name="tactic" value="burn" id="burn" />
                              <label for="burn">burn</label>
</div>

<div class="form-row multi">
  <span class="multi-label">Viking gear</span>
  <input type="checkbox" name="gear[helmet]" value="yes"
            id="helmet" checked="checked" /><label for="helmet">
                                  horned helmet</label>
  <input type="checkbox" name="gear[longboat]" value="yes"
            id="longboat" /><label for="pillage">longboat</label>
  <input type="checkbox" name="gear[goat]" value="yes" id="goat"
          checked="checked"/><label for="goat">magic goat</label>
</div>

<div class="form-row buttons">
  <input type="submit" id="submit" name="submit" value="Send" />
  <input type="button" id="more" name="more" value="More Options" />
</div>
</form>
```

To prepare the form for submission, we only need to call .ajaxForm() once, when the DOM is ready:

```
$(document).ready(function() {
  $('#test-form').ajaxForm({
    target: '.log'
  });
});
```

The user can then fill in the form fields:

When the **Send** button is later clicked, the server receives all of the form information without a browser refresh. For testing purposes, we can use PHP's print_r function to display the posted form contents:

```
Array
(
    [city] => Morton
    [state] => IL
    [comment] => Eric the Red is my hero!
    [villages] => 50
    [tactic] => pillage
    [gear] => Array
        (
            [helmet] => yes
            [longboat] => yes
        )

    [submit] => Send
)
```

If a callback is provided using the beforeSubmit option, the callback will be fired before the request is sent. The callback is passed the form data as returned by .formToArray(), the jQuery object that references the form, and the options object that was provided to .ajaxForm(). This callback is primarily useful for performing form validation:

```
$(document).ready(function() {
  $('#test-form').ajaxForm({
    target: '.ajax-form .log',
    beforeSubmit: function(formData, $form, options) {
      if ($form.find('#city').val() == '') {
        alert('You must enter a city.');
        return false;
      }
    }
  });
});
```

If a validation routine detects errors that the user must correct, the routine can return `false` to prevent the form from being submitted. In our example here, a value must be entered in the **City** field, or an alert will be shown and no submission will occur.

When a `dataType` is provided, the response data is interpreted accordingly. The processing performed is the same as with the `$.ajax` function, for the supported data types. Any `script` responses are interpreted as JavaScript and executed in the global context, while `json` responses are parsed as a JavaScript object or array. Calls that specify an `xml` data type do not cause any parsing to occur when the response is received.

If no `dataType` is provided, then we can instead use the `target` option. The DOM element referred to by the target will be filled with the response to the AJAX request, interpreted as plain HTML. The `dataType` and `target` options are mutually exclusive.

After any relevant processing has been performed due to the `dataType` or `target` options, the `success` callback is executed. This function is given the response data to act on. For information on ways to interpret and manipulate the response data, see the `$.ajax` function discussion in Chapter 7.

The `semantic` flag forces strict semantic ordering at the expense of execution speed. For more information, see the `.formToArray()` discussion later.

If `resetForm` or `clearForm` is set to `true`, the corresponding action will be taken before the `success` callback (if provided) is executed. For more information on these actions, see the `.clearForm` and `.resetForm` method discussions later.

If the form being submitted contains file upload fields, the file data will be properly uploaded using the `multipart/form-data` MIME type. No further action needs to be taken.

.ajaxFormUnbind()

> Restores a form to its non-AJAX state.
> .ajaxFormUnbind()

Parameters

None.

Return Value

The jQuery object, for chaining purposes.

Discussion

Calling .ajaxForm() on a form binds handlers to the submit event of the form and to the click events of any buttons and image inputs therein. If at a later time the form should no longer submit using AJAX, we can call .ajaxFormUnbind() on the same form to remove these handlers without disrupting any other handlers that may have been bound to the form elements.

Retrieving Form Values

These methods allow scripts to read and transform the values of fields in web forms.

.formToArray()

> Collects the values in a form into an array of objects.
> .formToArray([semantic])

Parameters

- semantic (optional): Whether to force strict HTML ordering of fields. The default value is false.

Return Value

An array of objects, each representing one field in the form.

Discussion

The .formToArray method fetches the values of a form, and organizes them into a data structure that is appropriate for passing to the jQuery AJAX functions such as $.ajax(), $.post(), and .load(). It can handle forms with any standard field type.

Given the form, illustrated in the `.ajaxFor()` discussion, the `.formToArray` method will return a JavaScript array of the form values:

```
[
    {name: city, value: Morton},
    {name: state, value: IL},
    {name: comment, value: Eric the Red is my hero!},
    {name: villages, value: 50},
    {name: tactic, value: pillage},
    {name: gear[helmet], value: yes},
    {name: gear[longboat], value: yes}
]
```

Each object in the array has a `name` and a `value` property. Checkbox elements that are not checked do not get represented in the array.

If the `semantic` argument is set to `true`, then the fields listed in the array will be guaranteed to be ordered as they are in the HTML source. If the form contains no `<input>` elements of type `image`, then this will already be the case. Avoid using this option unless it is needed, as the extra processing involved will slow down the method.

.formSerialize()

Collects the values in a form into a serialized string.

```
.formSerialize([semantic])
```

Parameters

- `semantic` (optional): Whether to force strict HTML ordering of fields. The default value is `false`.

Return Value

A string representation of the form fields, suitable for submission.

Discussion

The `.formSerialize` method fetches the values of a form, and converts them into a string that is appropriate for passing as a query string for a GET request. It can handle forms with any standard field type.

Given the form illustrated in the `.ajaxFor()` discussion, the `.formSerialize` method will return a string representation of the form values:

```
city=Morton&state=IL&comment=Eric%20the%20Red%20is%20my%20hero!
    &villages=50&tactic=pillage&gear%5Bhelmet%5D=yes
    &gear%5Blongboat%5D=yes
```

Each of the fields shows up as a key-value pair in the string. Checkbox elements that are not checked do not get represented in the string. The string is URL-encoded as necessary.

If the `semantic` argument is set to `true`, then the fields listed in the string will be guaranteed to be ordered as they are in the HTML source. If the form contains no `<input>` elements of type `image`, then this will already be the case. Avoid using this option unless it is needed, as the extra processing involved will slow down the method.

.fieldSerialize()

Collects the values of a set of fields into a serialized string.

> `.fieldSerialize([successful])`

Parameters
- `successful` (optional): Whether to prune the included field values to successful ones. The default value is `true`.

Return Value
A string representation of the form fields, suitable for submission.

Discussion
Like the `.formSerialize` method before it, the `.fieldSerialize` method fetches the values of a form, and converts them into a string that is appropriate for passing as a query string for a GET request. However, `.fieldSerialize()` acts on a jQuery object that references individual fields rather than the form as a whole.

It can handle fields of any standard type, such as `<select>` menus:

```
<select name="villages" id="villages">
  <option value="0">none</option>
  <option value="5" selected="selected">1-5</option>
  <option value="10">6-10</option>
  <option value="20">11-20</option>
  <option value="50">21-50</option>
```

```
    <option value="100">51-100</option>
    <option value="more">over 100</option>
</select>
```

The user can then select any option:

```
Villages sacked | 21-50      ▼ |
```

The value is pulled from the currently selected option, and the `.fieldSerialize` method will return a string representation of this value:

```
villages=50
```

Each of the given fields shows up as a key-value pair in the string. Checkbox elements that are not checked do not get represented in the string. The string is URL-encoded as necessary.

By default, fields are not represented in the string if they are not successful, as defined in the W3C specification for HTML forms:

```
http://www.w3.org/TR/html4/interact/forms.html#h-17.13.2
```

Successful fields are the ones that are submitted to the server during a normal form submission operation. For example, checkboxes that are currently checked are successful; unchecked ones are not. It is rare to want the values of unsuccessful fields, but if this is required, the `successful` parameter of `.fieldSerialize()` can be set to `false`.

Given the form illustrated in the `.ajaxFor()` discussion, `.fieldSerializer()` includes only checked radio buttons and checkboxes when `successful` is set to `true`:

```
tactic=loot&gear%5Bhelmet%5D=yes&gear%5Bgoat%5D=yes
```

But when successful is set to `false`, `fieldSerializer()` includes the unselected options as well:

```
tactic=loot&tactic=pillage&tactic=burn&gear%5Bhelmet%5D=yes
  &gear%5Blongboat%5D=yes&gear%5Bgoat%5D=yes
```

.fieldValue()

Collects the values of a set of fields into an array of strings.

```
.fieldValue([successful])

$.fieldValue(element[, successful])
```

Parameters (First Version)

- `successful` (optional): Whether to prune the included field values to successful ones. The default value is `true`.

Parameters (Second Version)

- `element`: The form input element whose value is to be retrieved.

- `successful` (optional): Whether to prune the included field values to successful ones. The default value is `true`.

Return Value

An array of strings containing the field values.

Discussion

The `.fieldValue()` method and the `$.fieldValue()` function both fetch the values of a form, returning them as an array of strings. The `.fieldValue()` method acts on a jQuery object that references individual fields, while the `$.fieldValue()` function performs the same task on the field element passed as its first parameter.

These operations can handle fields of any standard type, such as `<select>` menus:

```
<select name="villages" id="villages">
  <option value="0">none</option>
  <option value="5" selected="selected">1-5</option>
  <option value="10">6-10</option>
  <option value="20">11-20</option>
  <option value="50">21-50</option>
  <option value="100">51-100</option>
  <option value="more">over 100</option>
</select>
```

The user can then select any option:

The value is pulled from the currently selected option, and the `.fieldValue()` method will return an array representation of this value:

```
[50]
```

Each of the given fields shows up as a string in the array. Checkbox elements that are not checked do not get represented in the array.

By default, fields are not represented in the array if they are not successful, as defined in the W3C specification for HTML forms:

`http://www.w3.org/TR/html4/interact/forms.html#h-17.13.2`

Successful fields are the ones that are submitted to the server during a normal form submission operation. For example, checkboxes that are currently checked are successful; unchecked ones are not. It is rare to want the values of unsuccessful fields, but if this is required, the `successful` parameter of `.fieldValue()` can be set to `false`.

Given the form illustrated in the `.ajaxFor()` discussion, `.fieldValue()` includes only checked radio buttons and checkboxes when `successful` is set to to `true`:

    [loot, yes, yes]

But when `successful` is set to `false`, `.fieldValue()` includes the unselected options as well:

    [loot, pillage, burn, yes, yes, yes]

The `.fieldValue` method always returns an array; if there are no values to report in the set of elements being acted upon, the result array will be empty. In contrast, the `$.fieldValue` function will return `null` if the field element in question is not successful.

Form Manipulation

These methods allow scripts to easily change the current contents of a form on the page.

.clearForm()

Clears all data in a form.

    .clearForm()

Parameters

None.

Return Value

The jQuery object, for chaining purposes.

Discussion

This method finds all input fields (`<input>`, `<select>`, and `<textarea>` elements) within the matched elements, and clears their values. This method is usually applied to a `<form>` element, but can work with any container for fields (such as a `<fieldset>`) as well.

All fields are emptied, regardless of their default values:

The fields are cleared according to their type, as follows:

- Text fields and text areas have their values set to an empty string.
- Select elements are set to -1, which indicates no selection.
- Checkboxes and radio buttons are unchecked.
- Other fields, such as submit buttons and image inputs, are not affected.

Note that hidden fields are not affected by the clearing operation, even though they have a value.

.clearFields()

Clears all data in an input field.

```
.clearFields()
```

Parameters

None.

Return Value

The jQuery object, for chaining purposes.

Discussion

This method clears the values of all matched elements that are input fields (`<input>`, `<select>`, and `<textarea>` elements).

The `.clearFields` method differs from `.clearForm()` only in that `.clearForm()` is sent to a jQuery object that has matched the form element, while `.clearFields()` is sent to a jQuery object that matches the individual fields themselves:

The fields are cleared according to their type, as follows:

- Text fields and text areas have their values set to an empty string.
- Select elements are set to -1, which indicates "no selection."
- Checkboxes and radio buttons are unchecked.
- Other fields, such as submit buttons and image inputs, are not affected.

Note that hidden fields are not affected by the clearing operation, even though they have a value.

.resetForm()

Resets a form to its initial values.

        .resetForm()

Parameters

None.

Return Value

The jQuery object, for chaining purposes.

Discussion

This method returns all fields in a form to their initial values (the ones defined in the HTML source):

This action is accomplished using the DOM API's native .reset method. For this reason, .resetForm() can only be applied to a jQuery object that references <form> elements, unlike .clearForm(), which can be applied to jQuery objects referencing any containing element as well.

A
Online Resources

I can't remember what I used to know
Somebody help me now and let me go
— Devo,
"Deep Sleep"

The following online resources represent a starting point for learning more about jQuery, JavaScript, and web development in general, beyond what is covered in this book. There are far too many sources of quality information on the web for this appendix to approach anything resembling an exhaustive list. Furthermore, while other print publications can also provide valuable information, they are not noted here.

jQuery Documentation

jQuery Wiki

The documentation on jquery.com is in the form of a wiki, which means that the content is editable by the public. The site includes the full jQuery API, tutorials, getting started guides, a plug-in repository, and more:

```
http://docs.jquery.com/
```

jQuery API

On jQuery.com, the API is available in two locations — the documentation section and the paginated API browser.

The documentation section of jQuery.com includes not only jQuery methods, but also all of the jQuery selector expressions:

```
http://docs.jquery.com/Selectors
http://docs.jquery.com/
http://jquery.com/api
```

jQuery API Browser

Jörn Zaeferrer has put together a convenient tree-view browser of the jQuery API with a search feature and alphabetical or category sorting:

```
http://jquery.bassistance.de/api-browser/
```

Visual jQuery

This API browser designed by *Yehuda Katz* is both beautiful and convenient. It also provides quick viewing of methods for a number of jQuery plug-ins:

```
http://www.visualjquery.com/
```

Web Developer Blog

Sam Collet keeps a master list of jQuery documentation, including downloadable versions and cheat sheets, on his blog:

```
http://webdevel.blogspot.com/2007/01/jquery-documentation.html
```

JavaScript Reference

Mozilla Developer Center

This site has a comprehensive JavaScript reference, a guide to programming with JavaScript, links to helpful tools, and more:

```
http://developer.mozilla.org/en/docs/JavaScript/
```

Dev.Opera

While focused primarily on its own browser platform, *Opera's* site for web developers includes a number of useful articles on JavaScript:

```
http://dev.opera.com/articles/
```

Quirksmode

Peter-Paul Koch's Quirksmode site is a terrific resource for understanding differences in the way browsers implement various JavaScript functions, as well as many CSS properties:

```
http://www.quirksmode.org/
```

JavaScript Toolbox

Matt Kruse's JavaScript Toolbox offers a large assortment of homespun JavaScript libraries, as well as sound advice on JavaScript best practices and a collection of vetted JavaScript resources elsewhere on the Web:

```
http://www.javascripttoolbox.com/
```

JavaScript Code Compressors

Packer

This JavaScript compressor/obfuscator by *Dean Edwards* is used to compress the jQuery source code. It's available as a web-based tool or as a free download. The resulting code is very efficient in file size, at a cost of a small increase in execution time:

```
http://dean.edwards.name/packer/
http://dean.edwards.name/download/#packer
```

JSMin

Created by *Douglas Crockford*, *JSMin* is a filter that removes comments and unnecessary white space from JavaScript files. It typically reduces file size by half, resulting in faster downloads:

```
http://www.crockford.com/javascript/jsmin.html
```

Pretty Printer

This tool *prettifies* JavaScript that has been compressed, restoring line breaks and indentation where possible. It provides a number of options for tailoring the results:

```
http://www.prettyprinter.de/
```

(X)HTML Reference

W3C Hypertext Markup Language Home Page

The *World Wide Web Consortium* (*W3C*) sets the standard for (X)HTML, and the HTML home page is a great launching point for its specifications and guidelines:

```
http://www.w3.org/MarkUp/
```

CSS Reference

W3C Cascading Style Sheets Home Page

The W3C's CSS home page provides links to tutorials, specifications, test suites, and other resources:

```
http://www.w3.org/Style/CSS/
```

Mezzoblue CSS Cribsheet

Dave Shea provides this helpful *CSS cribsheet* in an attempt to make the design process easier, and provide a quick reference to check when you run into trouble:

```
http://mezzoblue.com/css/cribsheet/
```

Position Is Everything

This site includes a catalog of CSS browser bugs along with explanations of how to overcome them:

```
http://www.positioniseverything.net/
```

XPath Reference

W3C XML Path Language Version 1.0 Specification

Although jQuery's XPath support is limited, theW3C's *XPath Specification* may still be useful for those wanting to learn more about the variety of possible XPath selectors:

```
http://www.w3.org/TR/xpath
```

TopXML XPath Reference

The *TopXML* site provides helpful charts of axes, node tests, and functions for those wanting to learn more about XPath:

```
http://www.topxml.com/xsl/XPathRef.asp
```

MSDN XPath Reference

The *Microsoft Developer Network* website has information on XPath syntax and functions:

```
http://msdn2.microsoft.com/en-us/library/ms256115.aspx
```

Useful Blogs

The jQuery Blog

John Resig, et al., the official jQuery blog posts announcements about new versions and other initiatives among the project team, as well as occasional tutorials and editorial pieces.

```
http://jquery.com/blog/
```

Learning jQuery

Karl Swedberg, Jonathan Chaffer, Brandon Aaron, et al. are running a blog for jQuery tutorials, examples, and announcements:

```
http://www.learningjquery.com/
```

Jack Slocum's Blog

Jack Slocum, the author of the popular *EXT suite* of JavaScript components writes about his work and JavaScript programming in general:

```
http://www.jackslocum.com/blog/
```

Web Standards with Imagination

Dustin Diaz blog features articles on web design and development, with an emphasis on JavaScript:

```
http://www.dustindiaz.com/
```

Snook

Jonathan Snook's general programming/web-development blog:

```
http://snook.ca/
```

Wait Till I Come

Three sites by *Christian Heilmann* provide blog entries, sample code, and lengthy articles related to JavaScript and web development:

```
http://www.wait-till-i.com/
http://www.onlinetools.org/
http://icant.co.uk/
```

DOM Scripting

Jeremy Keith's blog picks up where the popular DOM scripting book leaves off—a fantastic resource for unobtrusive JavaScript:

```
http://domscripting.com/blog/
```

As Days Pass By

Stuart Langridge experiments with advanced use of the browser DOM:

```
http://www.kryogenix.org/code/browser/
```

A List Apart

A List Apart explores the design, development, and meaning of web content, with a special focus on web standards and best practices:

```
http://www.alistapart.com/
```

Particletree

Chris Campbell, Kevin Hale, and Ryan Campbell started a blog that provides valuable information on many aspects of web development:

```
http://particletree.com/
```

The Strange Zen of JavaScript

Scott Andrew LePera's weblog about JavaScript quirks, caveats, odd hacks, curiosities and collected wisdom. Focused on practical uses for web application development:

```
http://jszen.blogspot.com/
```

Web Development Frameworks Using jQuery

As developers of open-source projects become aware of jQuery, many are incorporating the JavaScript library into their own systems. The following is a brief list of some of the early adopters:

- Drupal: `http://drupal.org/`
- Joomla Extensions: `http://extensions.joomla.org/`
- Pommo: `http://pommo.org/`
- SPIP: `http://www.spip.net/`
- Trac: `http://trac.edgewall.org/`

For a more complete list, visit the *Sites Using jQuery* page at:

```
http://docs.jquery.com/Sites_Using_jQuery
```

B
Development Tools

When a problem comes along
You must whip it
                — Devo,
            "Whip It"

Documentation can help in troubleshooting issues with our JavaScript applications, but there is no replacement for a good set of software development tools. Fortunately, there are many software packages available for inspecting and debugging JavaScript code, and most of them are available for free.

Tools for Firefox

Mozilla Firefox is the browser of choice for the lion's share of web developers, and therefore has some of the most extensive and well-respected development tools.

Firebug

The *Firebug* extension for Firefox is indispensable for jQuery development:

```
http://www.getfirebug.com/
```

Some of the features of Firebug are :

- An excellent DOM inspector for finding names and selectors for pieces of the document
- CSS manipulation tools for finding out why a page looks a certain way and changing it
- An interactive JavaScript console
- A JavaScript debugger that can watch variables and trace code execution

Web Developer Toolbar

This not only overlaps Firebug in the area of DOM inspection, but also contains tools for common tasks like cookie manipulation, form inspection, and page resizing. You can also use this toolbar to quickly and easily disable JavaScript for a site to ensure that functionality degrades gracefully when the user's browser is less capable:

```
http://chrispederick.com/work/web-developer/
```

Venkman

Venkman is the official JavaScript debugger for the Mozilla project. It provides a troubleshooting environment that is reminiscent of the GDB system for debugging programs that are written in other languages.

```
http://www.mozilla.org/projects/venkman/
```

Regular Expressions Tester

Regular expressions for matching strings in JavaScript can be tricky to craft. This extension for Firefox allows easy experimentation with regular expressions using an interface for entering search text:

```
http://sebastianzartner.ath.cx/new/downloads/RExT/
```

Tools for Internet Explorer

Sites often behave differently in IE than in other web browsers, so having debugging tools for this platform is important.

Microsoft Internet Explorer Developer Toolbar

The *Developer* Toolbar primarily provides a view of the DOM tree for a web page. Elements can be located visually, and modified on the fly with new CSS rules. It also provides other miscellaneous development aids, such as a ruler for measuring page elements:

```
http://www.microsoft.com/downloads/details.
aspx?FamilyID=e59c3964-672d-4511-bb3e-2d5e1db91038
```

Microsoft Visual Web Developer

Microsoft's Visual Studio package can be used to inspect and debug JavaScript code:

```
http://msdn.microsoft.com/vstudio/express/vwd/
```

To run the debugger interactively in the free version (Visual Web Developer Express), follow the process outlined here:

```
http://www.berniecode.com/blog/2007/03/08/
how-to-debug-javascript-with-visual-web-developer-express/
```

DebugBar

The *DebugBar* provides a DOM inspector as well as a JavaScript console for debugging:

```
http://www.debugbar.com/
```

Drip

Memory leaks in JavaScript code can cause performance and stability issues for Internet Explorer. *Drip* helps to detect and isolate these memory issues:

```
http://Sourceforge.net/projects/ieleak/
```

Tools for Safari

Safari remains the *new kid on the block* as a development platform, but there are still tools available for situations in which code behaves differently in this browser than elsewhere.

Web Inspector

Nightly builds of Safari include the ability to inspect individual page elements and collect information especially about the CSS rules that apply to each one.

```
http://trac.webkit.org/projects/webkit/wiki/Web%20Inspector
```

Drosera

Drosera is the JavaScript debugger for Safari and other WebKit-driven applications. It enables breakpoints, variable watching, and an interactive console.

Other Tools

Firebug Lite

Though the Firebug extension itself is limited to the Firefox web browser, some of the features can be replicated by including the *Firebug Lite* script on the web page. This package simulates the Firebug console, including allowing calls to `console.log()` which usually causes JavaScript errors to be thrown in other browsers:

```
http://www.getfirebug.com/lite.html
```

TextMate jQuery Bundle

This extension for the popular Mac OS X text editor *TextMate* provides syntax highlighting for jQuery methods and selectors, code completion for methods, and a quick API reference from within your code. The bundle is also compatible with the *E* text editor for Windows:

```
http://www.learningjquery.com/2006/09/textmate-bundle-for-jquery
```

Charles

When developing AJAX-intensive applications, it can be useful to see exactly what data is being sent between the browser and the server. The *Charles* web debugging proxy displays all HTTP traffic between two points, including normal web requests, HTTPS traffic, Flash remoting, and AJAX responses:

```
http://www.xk72.com/charles/
```

Index

A

form events 118
keyboard events 124
mouse events 107

F

filtering methods
.contains() 43
.eq() 44
.filter() 40
.gt() 46
.lt() 45
.not() 42
Firefox tools
features, Firebug 239
Firebug 239
regular expressions test 240
Venkman 240
web developer toolbar 240
first-child 23
form, manipulating
.clearFields() 229
.clearForm() 228
.resetForm() 230
Form, plug-ins
about 215
AJAX form submissions 215
form, manipulating 228
form values, retrieving 223
form events
.blur() 119
.change() 120
.focus() 118
.select() 122
.submit() 123
form selectors
about 30
button 31
checkbox 31
checked 31
disabled form element 31
enabled form element 31
form elements 30
hidden 31
image button 31
password field 31
radio 31

reset button 31
submit button 31
text field 30
form values, retrieving
.fieldSerialize() 225
.fieldValue() 226
.formSerialize() 224
.formToArray() 223

G

general attributes
.attr() 63
.attr(attribute) 61
.removeAttr() 64
general sibling elements 21
global function
about 186
components in first version 186
components in second version 186
multiple functions 187
single functions 187

H

has attribute 28

I

implicit iteration 185
Internet Explorer tools
DebugBar 241
Drip 241
MS IE developer toolbar 240
MS Visual web developer 240

J

JavaScript compressors
JSMin 235
packer 235
pretty printer 235
JavaScript reference
dev.Opera 234
JavaScript toolbox 234
Mozilla developer center 234
Quirksmode 234

Printed in the United States
122179LV00010B/85/A

9 781847 193810